Terry:
Enjoy The
Rebel Magic!
Bob
#27

OVER-TIME

THE UNTOLD AND SURPRISING
STORY OF *THE REBELS*,
ONE OF CANADA'S LONGEST-LASTING
AMATEUR, ADULT HOCKEY TEAMS

WRITTEN BY

BOB FALCONI

 FriesenPress

Suite 300 - 990 Fort St
Victoria, BC, V8V 3K2
Canada

www.friesenpress.com

Copyright © 2021 by Bob Falconi
First Edition — 2021

Edited by Glynis Gibson, M.S.
Foreword by Joe Falconi

Bob "The Falcon" Falconi is one of the original Rebels players and has been with the team for all of its 50 years.

ISBN
978-1-5255-8229-5 (Hardcover)
978-1-5255-8230-1 (Paperback)
978-1-5255-8231-8 (eBook)

1. BIOGRAPHY & AUTOBIOGRAPHY, SPORTS

Distributed to the trade by The Ingram Book Company

TABLE OF CONTENTS

This book is dedicated to my children, Kim, Mark and Joe. They supported me throughout my zany ride with the Rebels. They, along with other Rebels offspring, became part of the larger Rebels family. They all respected us for who we were and what we did, and as they grew to be adults, they learned a few things from the Rebels: to always give 100%, to never quit; and to unceasingly push to overcome challenges and obstacles in their way. To this day, my children continue to make me proud of what they stand for and the lives they lead.

The book is also dedicated to all the players of any sport, male or female, who may never have made it to the pros but continue to play for the love of the game. You are winners who raise your own championship trophies every day.

A big thank-you to Joanne Falconi, for her support and encouragement in the journey of documenting and writing this book. Her help was immeasurable.

FORWARD

They called them "old-timers," but one would never consider them "old." My memories of the Rebels began when they were well into their "old-timer" years, but trust me when I say I've heard every story along the way…many times over. If it wasn't from my father, it was from one of the numerous others while at family parties, or sitting next to them in dressing rooms as I grew up. Over the years, I had many opportunities to not only watch them play, but to also share the ice with them…and the occasional beer. I can honestly say that these gents taught me a great deal about the game, teamwork, leadership and friendship. They were role models for a variety of reasons, both on and off the ice.

They had something that any young boy or athlete could admire—not simply their success on the ice, or the teamwork they exemplified, which was amazing in its own right—but it was the brotherhood and friendship that were to envy. They played hockey in the winter, softball and fastball in the summer, won championships and did everything as a tightknit group. They were not simply friends and teammates: They were much more than that—they were a family. Our families were so close that I grew up calling many of them "uncle" and their children "cousins." The relationship between the players went far beyond being on the same team, and this bled down into their families.

As a young boy playing hockey in the winter and lacrosse in the summer, I would look at these friendships my father had, and I would hope that one day I could have the same relationships with the groups I was in. And while I do have something similar with a handful of the individuals I grew up beside, none would compare to what this group developed over their 50 years…and certainly not as an entire team.

Perhaps a lot of this had to do with growing up when globalization and working abroad weren't as rampant as they are today. This certainly would have helped to keep the group together where today's generation might have been forced apart. Regardless, they had, and always will have, something special together, whether they are on the same soil or miles apart. The bond that formed between those that have worn the Rebels jersey has spanned generations, countries and decades for the large majority. Some call it "magic"— a special force that stemmed from the teamwork that began when the jerseys were put on and that extended long after the final buzzer sounded. Many years after that buzzer, in fact.

This type of team and teamwork was something that all good coaches would dream of achieving with their groups. It is the type of stuff that you typically only read about in books—the educational-style books about "effective teamwork" that people flock to books stores or online to buy to help them with the team they are coaching or their employees in their workplace. And if you had never seen it for yourself, you may even call it fiction. However, this was real. The Rebels were real. They were never on the front pages of newspapers or on prime-time TV, but this team was real for a select group of men, their families and their friends. It was real for 50 years, and it will be real for many years more, as their families carry on these traditions long after the final pair of skates are hung up for the last time.

For all intents and purposes, the Rebels were a dynasty. The team was put together on a whim for a singular purpose but evolved into something much greater than any one of the individuals involved could ever have imagined. They may, in fact, be the best team that was ever formed…that unfortunately will go unknown to most. The legacy that they have created is truly unique. Enjoy their story.

Joe Falconi, son of Bob Falconi

INTRODUCTION

For young boys with a dream in the 1950s and 1960s in Ontario, Canada, there were Saturday nights. They could listen to the Toronto Maple Leafs on the radio with their dads. They would hear the names of the famous players and imagine that one day they could be like them, streaking up the ice at Maple Leaf Gardens, crossing the blue line and winding up for a slap shot. The famous voice of Foster Hewitt, one of the first hockey broadcasters in Canada, would boom over the radio, "He shoots, he scores!" The building would erupt and the fans would go wild. They would be the envy of all of Canada. The next day, their picture would be plastered on the sports pages, and they would be a hero from coast to coast.

If you were born in 1946 and grew up in a small Ontario town, your career choices were limited. Most boys saw their fathers working in low-wage labour jobs. They saw the daily grind of trudging off to work in the morning, lunchbox in hand, and returning at night, exhausted from spending nine hours in a sweatshop. Even though the job broke men down, it was what they had to do to pay the bills and support their wives and children. Back then, the thought of a rewarding, fulfilling job was unheard of. Men worked hard for their paychecks, and their reward was putting food on their tables and roofs over their heads. They supported their families and didn't question anything. This cycle was hard to break.

During that time, there could be no better life for an athletic boy than to grow up to be a superstar in the NHL. For most, it was an ambition and a dream—a dream that was always taunting them.

The ice surfaces at the parks were full of very talented boys who could skate like the wind and shoot a puck like it had been fired out of a cannon. If you were lucky, your dad would build you a rink in your backyard and stick lights on a post so you could play until bedtime. If not, a frozen corner of a river or creek would suffice. You could play shinny with your buddies to keep the dream alive. Every day you would play the game emulating your idol. You would fantasize about the fame, riches, big houses, fast cars and beautiful women that awaited those who made it. What Canadian boy didn't want that life? It was the Canadian dream.

The life of a pro athlete—specifically, of a pro hockey player—was the envy of most young boys. Never did it occur to them that realizing the dream might not lead to the perfect life. No one ever thought there could be a dark side. Surely being good enough to make it to the NHL meant that life would be great. It would mean the end of the lunchbox cycle.

Very few actually made it, however, and for some who did, the dream became a nightmare. No doubt one of the most famous nightmares is the story of Derek Sanderson. In his biography, "Crossing the Line: The Outrageous Story of a Hockey Original," Sanderson recounts his rise and fall from hockey grace.

Born in 1946 in a small town in Ontario, he was a young, talented, driven boy who also dreamed of making it to the NHL. In his case, the dream became a reality. Not only was he one of the few who made it, he also ascended to the top. While playing for the Boston Bruins, Sanderson was named the NHL's 1967-1968 Rookie of the Year, and a couple of years later, he hoisted the coveted Stanley Cup. He was rich. He was famous. He was living the dream.

In 1972, he was persuaded to jump from the NHL to the new World Hockey Association and signed a contract with the Philadelphia Blazers that made him the highest paid athlete in the world at that time. He had risen to the very top; he had it all. But his dream soon became a nightmare.

Sanderson's tenure with the Blazers was disastrous. He was a notorious partier, with booze, drugs and women near-constant companions. Injuries limited his play to only eight games. By the end of the season, the Blazers bought out his contract for $1 million. He returned to the Bruins, which still owned his NHL rights, and was traded.

Injuries, alcohol addiction and lavish living marred the rest of his short-lived career, and he ended up losing everything: his money, his career, his business, his friends and his dignity. Instead of living in a posh penthouse in Boston, he lived on the streets of New York City. Instead of fighting for the puck, he fought drunks for a warm spot to sleep in Central Park. Instead of stealing the puck from the opposition and scoring a short-handed goal (for which he was renowned in the NHL), he stole bottles of booze from sleeping drunks' pockets.

Sanderson wasn't the only one to fall. Many hockey players and athletes from other sports who seemingly made it discovered that rising to the pinnacle of athletic success did not guarantee a happy, wonderful life.

Those who make it to the sports summit are a small part of the population. According to hockeycanada.ca, in a 1985 study of all 10-year-olds playing organized hockey in the province (22,000 to be exact) by Jim Parcels, a 13-year veteran of minor and junior hockey in Ontario, only 105 made it to the Ontario Junior Hockey League (OHLL), and only 42 others received scholarships to NCAA Division I schools in the U.S. This means that only 132 of those 22,000 made it to the top NHL feeder leagues. Of those 132, only 15 played at least one season in the NHL. That's .68 percent of the original 22,000. The funnel to the top is very narrow.

For most average, or even above average, boys who are looking to make it to the big leagues, there comes a time when they are told, "No." In the '50s and '60s, usually the bad news would come in a smoke-filled office in some arena where a coach would sit you down and give you the "not enough" speech. You know the one: "You're not big enough," "…fast enough," or "…dedicated enough." Then you would be cut from the team. The dream would come to a disappointing end. You would leave wondering what happened; in your mind, you were as good as the others.

There was a lot of truth to that sentiment. A fine line existed between those who became stars and those who envied them. Of course, the great ones were easy to spot. At the same time, however, there were a lot of journeymen hockey players who made the NHL, but weren't destined for stardom. Perhaps they only played a game or a season, or maybe they had a lengthy career and never became stars. But still, their dream of making it to the big league had come true.

Today the dream has become even bigger. By the beginning of the 21st century, top athletes reached superstar status. Currently countless athletes are paid massive amounts of money to play, and unlike during the '50s and the '60s, kids have opportunities in many more sports than just the big four of hockey, football, basketball and baseball. There is tennis, swimming, golf, car racing and soccer, just to name a few, where athletes are earning substantial pay days.

While it is not any easier to get to the top today, there is a lot of pressure to do so. Nowadays coaches teach kids about conditioning, nutrition and strategies to help them become better athletes. Sport psychologists work with their minds to ensure they are mentally prepared to compete. Unfortunately, by the time many kids have the "not enough" chat, they are burned out and are ready to give up the game. It's a shame that our culture puts so much emphasis on making it to the pros that it seems to have forgotten why athletes play in the first place.

Every once in a while, however, there are cherished glimpses of athletes who are there simply for the love of the game. The 1988 Winter Olympics in Calgary, Canada, captured the imaginations of spectators globally as they cheered for two underdogs: Michael Edwards and the Jamaican bobsled team.

Michael Edwards, who became known as "Eddie the Eagle," was an English skier who became the first competitor since 1928 to represent Great Britain in Olympic ski jumping. The Jamaican bobsled team represented a tropical nation in a winter sport. Even though both clearly were not good enough to medal, and in fact finished last in their respective competitions, the world rooted for them, loving their spirit, enthusiasm and love of their sports.

Much is made about the ones who get there, and much is made about the fallen stars like Derek Sanderson. Little is heard about the ones who almost made it. What happened to them? What happened to their dreams? For those who aren't "good enough," the game should not have to end in a smoke-filled office.

Fortunately there are some who continue to play long after their dreams have been dashed. The Rebels Hockey Club out of Mississauga, Ontario, is a good example.

The Rebels are a group of ordinary guys who never made it, but in 1969 established their own hockey team and continued to play competitive hockey for forty-six years, not for fame or fortune, but because they loved it. After finishing their competitive playing the men continued the friendship and camaraderie by continue to golf together, socialize together and even put on the skates for a friendly scrimmage. In 2019, the team celebrated 50 years of fellowship! That's half a century of lacing up their skates simply because they love the game and the fun associated with it.

The Rebels have set the record for the longest lasting "team of ordinary guys" in Canadian hockey history. Their journey is one of inspiration, dedication, commitment, camaraderie and fun. While their names may not be recognized, if dedication, passion and will to win mean anything, their story should be heard. This is their story.

CHAPTER 1

CRAZY HARRY

Born in 1947 and living in downtown Toronto, Harry, too, had the dream. As a son of immigrants, he knew all too well the effort and hard work it took to raise a family. Life was not easy for his parents: They worked in hard labour jobs trying to make ends meet. His dad was employed at Avro Canada, the maker of the Avro Arrow jet, and his mom worked at General Electric. For entertainment on Saturday nights, Harry would listen to the Maple Leafs on the radio.

His immigrant parents did not understand Harry's love for sports. "Harry," they would say, "you go to school and get a good education so you have a better life than me." As Harry played in the parks with his buddies, however, the dream grew.

The parks and rinks would have some tough guys who would steal your puck, or force you to the corners to play, so they could play their game in the middle of the ice and have the nets to themselves. You had to earn respect to scrimmage on the crowded, outdoor ice. Many boys just went home or played ball hockey in the laneway not wanting to fight for a spot on the ice.

Not Harry! He learned at a young age that life was not about negotiation, but about survival. Get pushed around on the ice, and you'll get pushed around the rest of your life. That was not for him. So he played and he battled. As he grew into a teen, he developed into a very good, rough-and-tough athlete who could handle any situation.

Hockey was only one of the sports in which he excelled. Football was the other. As he entered Humberside High School, he had to learn to balance his academic life with playing football and hockey and working at a part-time job while trying to have some sort of social life with his friends, especially the girls. His parents pushed him on academics while his athletic drive pushed him toward sports.

Harry was a gifted athlete playing on one of the dominant teams in high school football and leading his Humberside Huskies team to two city championships in five years. He also was a formidable force playing high school hockey and served as captain of the squad.

Some would say that the only thing that kept Harry out of the pros was his craziness. He had it all but just wouldn't help himself. Most found it hard to understand what drove him. Harry loved to be different, and he loved to live on the edge.

On a rainy fall day, his high school football team was practicing on their muddy field at the back of the school. Harry was always carrying the ball so he was in the thick of the mud for most of the practice. When it ended, the coach told the players to make sure their uniforms were washed and ready for the game the next day. Since his mother was a hardworking woman, the last thing Harry wanted to do was present a muddy uniform for her to deal with. Unfortunately, he knew nothing about washing clothes.

As Harry entered the school from the practice field, covered in mud from head to toe, he heard a commotion coming from the pool area. He saw that a women's synchronized swimming competition was taking place. Teams from all over Toronto were competing for the high school championship.

Sporting his muddy uniform, Harry jumped into the deep end of the pool in the middle of the competing swimmers. Was it because he thought it was not fair for the coach to ask his mother to clean a muddy uniform after she worked like a slave all day? Or was it Harry just being Harry?

Of course, he didn't realize that the dirt in the pool would force the competition to end, and when he sat with the principal the next day, before being expelled for a week, he argued that he thought this was the easiest way to get rid of the mud and that he had no malicious intent. The principal, unfortunately, didn't see it Harry's way.

When Harry graduated from high school in 1968, he was heavily recruited to play football by the University of Toronto. The coach said he had a good chance at a starting position on a team that had won the championship the previous year. The championship U of T team was young and did not lose any first-stringers to graduation, however, so Harry felt the odds of a rookie playing were slim.

But a great school with a fabulous football program was too tempting to turn down, so Harry accepted the invitation and during practices did what he was good at: He worked hard and toughed it out against the other guys. He so impressed the coaching staff that he played his way onto the team and beat out a veteran player for a first-string position.

The team went undefeated in regular season play and was heavily favoured going into the playoffs. Its first-round opponent was Queens University. U of T had played Queens twice in the regular season and had won both times.

In the final game of the regular season, Harry broke his arm in two places and could not play in the opening round. Nevertheless, he accompanied the team to Kingston where the game was to be played.

Harry was a very popular player. Over the season, others came to respect his athletic ability as well as his dynamic and strange sense of humour. His quick wit and intelligence made him a favourite with all the players. Before curfew the night prior to the Queens playoff game, Harry invited a few of the players, including U of T's all-star quarterback, to his room to play cards. Suddenly Harry's door burst open, and five girls with two cases of beer came in.

The party lasted late into the night. After all, they were only playing Queens and it would be an easy game. (Harry later said that he insisted that the players honour the curfew, but no one listened.)

The next day, however, U of T was upset by the inferior Queens team. The press described U of T's effort as lackluster because they took Queens for granted. The coach was furious. When he found out about the late-night party, Harry became the scapegoat and was banned from university sports for life. Some players from Harry's team were not as gifted as he was, yet they went on to play professional football. What determines the ones who make it and the ones who don't? Does the cream always rise to the top, or does destiny put the unlucky ones in the wrong place at the wrong time?

Harry then focused his sport recreation on hockey. A fast skater with a blistering slap shot, Harry had played most of his hockey in high school, and back then, the quality of high school hockey rivaled that of the non-school leagues. The non-school Toronto Hockey League (THL) was where young, elite hockey players would play. Area high schools would allow their students to play in the THL as well as for the school team, and as such, high school hockey was extremely good and quite competitive.

The Toronto area also had senior men's leagues where men would come together from various parts of the city to play. In the late '60s, the Lambton Senior League, which was in the west end of Toronto, was comprised of men who had played very good hockey and still wanted to play the game. It had six teams with players who had played hockey at the junior A or B levels and some at the semi-pro level. Teams even had former pros who still wanted to play, but were at the end of their career.

Unfortunately, the men's leagues also were usually goon leagues where the games became a scene from the movie "Slap Shot" which featured vicious hockey playing. The men's league games, simply put, were violence on ice.

In minor hockey leagues and school leagues, where young boys and teens played, there were controls, rules and effective disciplinary measures that were employed to keep things from getting out of hand. The pro leagues had the same. The senior leagues, however, usually were governed by current or former players. Most were considered outlaw leagues, and there was a survival-of-the-fittest mentality. The rules and disciplines were in place but there was no way to effectively penalize the deviants. If a game got out of hand, it was up to the referee to try and keep things in order, but most leagues had difficulty finding referees willing to officiate because they feared for their own safety.

In the senior leagues, players had to earn respect or they would, quite literally, be run out of the league. Toughness as a player or as a team was critical. This hockey was not for everyone, and many young players who did not make it to a higher level of hockey would quit the game after their minor hockey league careers came to an end.

As a teenager, Harry was as strong as any man, and in 1968, after he had been banned from university sports, he was invited to play in a senior men's league outside the school system: the unexceptional Riverside Sunoco team, which consisted mostly of mediocre players with an average age of 28. Harry, who was still a teen, was by far the superior player.

The best team in the league, Bodding Pumping, had a number of former semi-professional players. The team had a reputation for being dirty and physical, and the players enjoyed humiliating their competition on the scoreboard while punishing them physically on the ice. The team's best player was Gary G (he will be known only as Gary G), who played semi-pro hockey and was a gifted goal scorer, but was considered a very dirty hockey player.

Near the end of Harry's first season with Riverside Sunoco, during a game against Bodding Pumping, Gary and Harry were at each other's throats, and they would not back down from one another. Harry did not have a lot of support from his teammates, whereas Gary had a team of tough bullies backing him up.

Senior men's games did not draw many fans other than a few parents and family members. Gary's wife was in attendance at this particular game, and throughout it she was yelling at Harry and encouraging her husband, "Get him, get that jerk!"

Near the end of the game, Harry scored a goal. Bodding was well in the lead and the game was pretty much over, but as Harry rounded the net with his hands up in typical hockey celebratory fashion, a few of the Bodding players took a run at him. Gary was in the middle of the posse. Harry was speared in the chest and went down hard, spitting blood from his mouth. He was in trouble. No teammates came to Harry's defense. An ambulance was called, and as Harry was taken off the ice on a stretcher, someone from the stands threw a full cup of hot coffee at him.

Harry had incurred a punctured lung and spent two weeks in the hospital recovering from his injury.

Many guys at this juncture would have walked away and looked to play somewhere else. Others might have given up the game entirely. Not Harry. He knew that if he backed away from this, he would crawl forever, and he vowed revenge.

CHAPTER 2

CALLING ALL REBELS

That summer, prior to the 1969 hockey season, Harry called on three of his closest high school friends: Joe Pfaff, Wayne "Texan" Magee and Rick "Carrot" McArthur. Harry asked them to help put together a team of the best hockey players they could find to compete in the Lambton League as a new team. Their objective was to assemble a team that could play the game yet handle the rough stuff, too. Harry also told them what happened with Gary G. They were like brothers, so his friends agreed to help Harry seek his vengeance.

Joe and Wayne were the nucleus around which they would build the team. Both of them were good hockey players and very tough. Both were natural athletes, and hockey was not the only sport in which they excelled. Joe was a star second baseman who, as a Canadian, had a tryout with the Kansas City Royals. (Canadians had to be exceptional baseball players to get looked at by the pros.) Wayne was a star football player who held a number of high school records who was recruited by the University of South Dakota. Rick was a brilliant coach and recruiter of talent. (Later in life, Rick would be one of Canada's top volleyball coaches and instructed many of Canada's Olympic volleyball players.) He would add much to the organization and management of the team.

The four of them were on a mission. They recruited friends, such as Gordie Chalmers, a slick left-winger. Next was Tony Caransi, a very tough and physical scrapper who could duke it out with anyone who dared. Along with Tony came his brother, Mario, who was a big, strong right-winger. They brought their cousin, Terry Lavarou, another strong, talented winger.

Then came Brian "Smitty" Smith, who had played with Harry on the Sunoco team. Another smooth left-winger who could skate like the wind, Smitty was an anomaly for a hockey player, as he was born with only one hand. His right arm was complete but had just a stub where a hand should have been. Smitty, however, wanted no sympathy from anyone. He was a well-tuned athlete who loved to compete and win. Physically, he was built like a rock. As opposing players soon found out, when they annoyed him, he would "stump" them, and getting stumped by Smitty was like running into the end of a baseball bat! Another player invited from the Sunoco team was Sid Thompson. He was a big high scoring forward who as a teen was the scoring leader in the Lampton League. Sid was also a star in high school hockey for Western Tech in Toronto.

Harry, Joe, Wayne and Rick knew that high school teams had many more good players. Since they had competed against these teams for years, they knew whom to select. They approached players they knew would help them meet their goals. Johnny "Johnny B Good" Good, John "JC" Cottrell and Tom Bolko were added from Western Tech. Johnny Good was a gifted sniper and great playmaker. JC was an outstanding offensive defenceman who could quarterback the game from his defensive position. Tom Bolko also was a great skater and goal sniper.

Rick Osbourne, a tall, strong, tough winger from the Humberside Huskies, and I, Bob "The Falcon" Falconi from Harbord Collegiate, an offensive-minded defenceman, were added to the team. Finally, Glen Patterson, a goalie from Humberside Huskies, was tapped to mind the cage. Roy Hysen an alternate goalie was added as well. Roy, had a hearing impediment and years later would be the coach of Canada's National Hockey Team for the hearing impaired.

The players had a lot of apprehension about joining the team. Most of them were bitter rivals, having battled against each other for years, and the thought of playing together was mind-boggling. As the men prepared for the first practice, they were extremely tense, and the dressing room was silent. Their competitiveness was palpable, and when they hit the ice, they tried to outdo each other. It was a powder keg about to explode.

When it looked like it an explosion was imminent, Rick called all the guys together to centre ice. He explained that they were putting together the best senior team that had ever been assembled. "We are embarking on the road to immortality, and we are building something that has never been done before. This will be an adventure, and you guys are the nucleus of future greatness."

With that, Crazy Harry (a nickname that stuck), let out a giant yawn and wryly asked Rick what book he read that from. In his usual manner, Harry broke the ice and the tension melted.

Before long the team started to gel, and in September 1969, the Rebels were born. This was to be Harry's team, and its objective was simple: be the dominant senior team in the Lambton League.

Most of the new recruits did not know about Harry's ulterior motive yet, but they heard the Gary story a few weeks into the season. In a strange way, Harry's call to justice was what initially bonded the Rebels. Each player could relate to Harry's desire for revenge because they all had their own scores to settle with the likes of the "Garys" in their own hockey lives.

The Rebels quickly established themselves in the league. The first two games of the season were against weaker teams, and the Rebels were convincing victors. The third game was against a team sponsored by Bell Telephone. They were a tough team that had lost to Bodding in the finals the previous year. Since then they had strengthened their team with more experienced players, and they were looking forward to teaching the young upstart Rebels a lesson.

During the warmup, as the teams were skating around, a few of the Bell players tried to intimidate the Rebels by taunting them. "Hey, punks, the stretchers are on ready, better keep your heads up." Their laughter and taunts continued until Tony Caranci had enough. As the referees whistled for the opening faceoff, Tony grabbed the first Bell player he could reach and started throttling him. Centre ice became a battle ground. All the Rebels' heavyweights were pounding the Bell players. This was all before the game even started! The Rebels made a statement: They were the new sheriffs in town. When the game finally began, only a few players were left on both teams, as most had been tossed out of the game. Bell's team was no match for the remaining Rebels.

The Rebels passed the first test and were now recognized as a force in the league.

As mentioned before, the referee in senior hockey has a thankless job. It is like being a skunk at a garden party. The Lambton League, however, was quite fortunate. It had two extremely devoted and respected referees, George Moore and Dave Montgomery, who enjoyed refereeing the games every week. Two sensational guys who got to know the players and earned everyone's respect, Moore and Montgomery were able to keep the games under control for the most part, despite the players' antics. The teams knew that without them, the league would not exist. Montgomery would comment in later years that he had no idea how he and Moore kept the league under control and the games safe, but the players knew it was because of their rapport with the players and respect that they built through the years. No one challenged their authority. They were the bosses.

After the disaster between the Rebels and Bell, and knowing that the showdown between the Rebels and Bodding was coming up, Moore and Montgomery developed a plan to prevent another one from taking place. So prior to the Rebels vs. Bodding game, Moore and Montgomery visited the Rebels' dressing room and introduced themselves to each player. Then they approached Harry and acknowledged that they were aware of the unfortunate injury he had suffered the previous year, and they vowed that they would not tolerate that kind of behaviour from the Bodding team or any other team. They asked Harry not to do anything stupid that could result in another bad injury to him or any of the opposing players. Harry listened and promised he would behave, but everyone knew that he had been waiting for this moment for over a year. Harry was going to make Gary pay the price, and the Rebels stood strong behind him.

The showdown had arrived. It was obvious as the game started that things were different this time around. Gary was apprehensive. He knew that Harry had the backing of a bunch of tough guys who would not give an inch. Whenever Harry went on the ice, Gary would immediately jump off. Harry taunted him a few times and invited him to play a shift against him. But Gary would not budge from the bench. Even the other Bodding players did not want to engage the Rebels, and the much-anticipated showdown turned out to be an easy Rebels victory.

The Rebels were thrilled, Moore and Montgomery were happy, but Harry was clearly upset. In the dressing room, Harry suggested that Gary was nothing but a coward. The guys on the team told Harry to calm down as he had made his point. The Rebels were No. 1 in the league, and that was Harry's best revenge. But Harry didn't buy it. First place was not a fair exchange for two weeks in a hospital.

The next week, Bodding and Gary were to play Club 17, another top team in the league. Club 17, hearing about the Rebels joining the league, had revamped their team, and they were a strong contender for the top spot. Harry and the other Rebels decided to go watch the game. Coincidentally, they were seated close to Gary's mother and wife.

While the game was a close, rough encounter, Harry continually taunted Gary from the stands and seemed to be enjoying himself knowing that his insults could be heard by Gary's mother and, particularly, his wife. Harry believed that Gary's wife was the one who tossed hot coffee on him as he was on the stretcher. There weren't many people in the stands, so every word could be clearly heard. Harry had a brilliant mind and a great sense of humour. No one could ever take Harry on in a war of words because they would simply be outgunned. He had a comeback line for anything thrown his way. Although he was as tough as they came, his jokester ways were legendary. When Harry was on a roll, no one could shut him down.

Nearing the end of the game, Gary was involved in a skirmish on the ice and was penalized for his infraction. This was Harry's chance to really let him have it, and he unleashed a verbal barrage as Gary made his way to the penalty box.

No one was really sure how old Gary's mother was. The team thought she might have been in her 60s. A tiny lady, she obviously loved her son, but no one anticipated what happened next. (Keep in mind Harry was a handsome, muscular 20-year-old.) After one of Harry's taunts, Gary's mom fearlessly stood up, turned around, gave a fiery glare and screamed, "Harry, if you don't shut up, I am going to come up there and personally give you the spanking you deserve!"

The rink went silent. Even Gary, who was in the penalty box, heard the comment and was dumbfounded. Harry seemed at a loss for words. The Rebels knew Harry was way too much of a gentleman to say anything nasty to her. Had Gary's mother put Harry in his place?

As "Mrs. Gary" triumphantly sat down with a smirk on her face, Harry stood up. Oh, no! What was he about to do? Time was suspended as everyone was on edge waiting to see what Harry would do or say.

All of a sudden Harry yelled for everyone to hear, "Hey Gary, better strap the skates on your mother. She has more balls than you do!"

Even "Mrs. Gary" couldn't withhold her laughter. Crazy Harry had his revenge, complete and sweet!

CHAPTER 3

BUILDING THE REBELLION

Harry's original intention was to even the score with Gary. Once he realized what he had assembled, however, he focused on establishing the Rebels as the Lambton League's powerhouse. He knew that Rick, Joe, Wayne and he had built something special, and he wanted it to continue. This was not an ordinary team: This was a group of elite players who were enjoying playing together. They were dedicated and committed. They had something that they had not seen in any team they had ever played for. There was a certain magic to this group of young men. The team had a destiny.

The Rebels won the league championship in their first year and established a record for most wins in a single season. Harry and the team were pleased but not yet content. They knew they were good, but they wanted to build on their success and become the most dominant team ever in senior hockey. So Harry and Rick started recruiting again.

Over the next couple of years, they added key players to the team. First they added the Robb brothers. Rick was a solid right winger. He had a bullet of a wrist shot and could pick the upper corner of any net before the goalie had a chance to move. A defensive specialist, he would shut down the top players on the other teams through his grit and tenacity. He made an art of hacking and slashing opposing players out of sight of the referee. His rat-like play and harassment of the opposition made him a force in the league.

His brother, Barry, was a smooth stick handler, making a name for himself in the Queensway Minor Hockey League in Etobicoke, Ontario. His play was compared to the legendary Gordie Howe. An effortless skater, Barry was a superb, shifty skater and an unselfish playmaker. His stickhandling of the puck was a joy to watch.

Steve Taylor and his younger brother, Bobby, were added next. Steve was a rock-solid, mean, tough defenceman, while Bobby was a gifted skater and goal scorer. In the case of Steve and Bobby, the apple did not fall far from the tree, with both being tremendous athletes and competitors. Their father, Harley Taylor, a well-respected coach in the Toronto Marlie organization, ensured Steve and Bobby knew how to play the game. Harley was an accomplished athlete who excelled as a fastball pitcher. While growing up in North Bay, Ontario, he had the opportunity to pitch against Eddie Feigner and his crew, aka, "King and his Court." Harley and his North Bay team were one of only a few teams ever to beat the legendary King.

Steve and Bobby brought with them another young sniper named Brian Cater, who gave the Rebels a scoring combination that was unmatched. While Steve anchored the blue line, Bobby and Brian were unstoppable scoring machines.

Joining the team to man the net was Doug Handy, a young, outstanding goalie from the Provincial Junior A league. An all-star goalie in junior hockey, Doug had tiger-like reflexes. Goaltending was going through a transition in the '70s, as goalies had to be better skaters and much more nimble in goal. Gone were the days when the goalie stood in his crease hoping to get hit by the puck. Doug moved like a cat and baffled opponents with his speed, exemplifying the new era of mobile hockey goaltenders. Getting through an iron door was easier than scoring on him.

Bob Sidey and John Bostock rounded out the defence. Both were high school prodigies who were not afraid to tangle with anyone. After high school, Bob played Pro hockey in Europe before coming back to Canada and going to Laurentian University. Later he went to University of Toronto where he played with the Blues. There he teamed up with John who had just returned from a tryout with the NHL's California Golden Seals team. They were sturdy, tough competitors who had great university careers. They split their time playing with the Rebels and some classic Blues teams. Both would eventually have tryouts with the Toronto Maple Leafs under legendary coach Tom Watts.

Gord Kenwood, a stocky power forward, joined the Rebels next. Gord was built like a Sherman tank. With his immense strength serving as a force on the ice, he owned the corners of the rink. As a gifted football player, he had been a final cut from the Montreal Alouettes Canadian Football League team before joining the Rebels. Gord was a linebacker who delivered punishing tackles. On the ice he traded tackles for body checks.

Gord became a legend with the Rebels during a game at Double Rink Arenas in Vaughan. The opposing team had a player who had a reputation for being mean and dirty. A big, solid guy, he used his stick like a spear. Soft-spoken, Gord would go about his business in a quiet manner, but he would not tolerate cheap shots. During one game, Gord had cautioned the other guy to keep his stick under control. During one of the faceoffs, the big guy stuck his stick into Barry Robb's face and viciously sliced him. This was not an accident. Gord was not on the ice at the time, but he stood on the boards and called the guy out. That left him no choice but to come to the bench and challenge Gord. His first mistake was spearing Barry; his second was coming to the bench. Gord, who was half the other guy's size, flew off the boards like Superman and proceeded to pummel him. Later that day, Gord checked on Barry, who had received nine stitches, to make sure he was OK. That was the spirit that embodied the Rebels.

Mike Tilley, a tall, smooth-skating winger, joined as a sniper on the forward line. A gifted athlete, Mike was continually one of the top scorers in the league. He was nicknamed "Hollywood" because his long, blond hair would flow from under his helmet as he streaked up the ice. If the Rebels ever sold a hockey calendar, like firemen did, Mike would have been on the cover because of his looks. He was also a highly touted fastball pitcher and combined with Steve Mauthe (who joined the Rebels a few years later) as the best pitching combination in the Ontario Sr. Baseball Association.

Completing the forward lines were three other solid additions to the team: Randy Curran, Les Gouge and Steve Zavislak.

Randy was a smooth-skating, goal-producing forward who developed his skills playing with the newly formed Toronto Young Nationals Junior A team. He was a top scorer with the Young Nats.

Les played minor hockey in Toronto and was a strong forward. All muscle, he was a fitness guru, and his strength and tireless skating made him a big asset to the team.

Steve was a product of the Weston Dodgers Junior B system. He was also a gifted baseball player and signed a minor league contract with the Detroit Tigers. He played for two years with them before joining the Rebels as a big, intimidating forward.

Another standout addition was Ernie Campe. A high school hockey player for Harbord, CI, Ernie went on a scholarship to the University of Minnesota, Duluth. He was a star defenceman for the university for four years. After he graduated from Duluth, he was a top draft choice for the Montreal Canadiens. As the Canadiens were solid on defense at the time with Serge Savard, Guy Lapointe, Jacques Laperrière and Larry Robinson, Ernie played a year in their farm system in Des Moines, Iowa.

By year three of the building process, the Rebels became the team that Harry and Rick envisioned. They were fast, strong and solid all over the ice. If opposing teams wanted to rough it up, the Rebels would respond. If other teams stuck to hockey, the Rebels would school them. They had great scoring power, solid defence and an unbeatable goalie. Other teams in the league did everything possible to try to beat them, but the Rebels were just too strong.

As good and unified as they were on the ice, they were the same off the ice. They played together and partied together. They were a family. Rick and Harry knew what skills were needed for a team to be good and win games, but they had wanted to create something bigger than just a winning team of teens and young men. The result of their vision even surprised themselves, as they had built something much bigger than a competitive hockey team. They knew by their careful selections of the right kind of hockey players with iconic personalities that they had built something that would last through time. This was a different kind of team, and one that had something very special.

A manager of hockey leagues and arenas in Mississauga, Ontario, observed that in the Mississauga Senior Hockey League, the average adult hockey team had a life expectancy of approximately three years. While professional and university teams as well as youth hockey organizations naturally pass the test of time, adult recreational teams do not last long before the players tire of each other or cannot raise the funds required to play. Because of the physical and organizational demands, senior hockey teams do not survive very long.

Harry and Rick knew that their players had to be good on the ice, but they also had to have the right kind of inner strength, personality and determination to stand the test of time. Rick did most of the recruiting, and Harry put the players through the character test. Harry would ridicule, taunt and joke about the team players and their abilities, or lack thereof. Harry was ruthless and non-selective about where, when, how and whom he would put to the test. Those who lasted on the team would either laugh with Harry or be man enough to hold his own and push back. If players couldn't do either, their days with the Rebels were numbered.

Harry was one of the best guys in the world to have on your team, once you knew how to handle him. The Rebels were his family. He would choose whom to keep, and whom to discard. His decision making was never questioned.

Most senior hockey teams eventually fall apart because of lack of money. Hockey is an expensive game with the cost to enter leagues, pay referees and rent practice ice. Ernie would often joke, "In Duluth I had people carry my equipment and make sure everything was laid out and clean prior to me entering the dressing room. Now I have to pay to play!"

To raise money for the team in the early years, the Rebels hosted stag parties. These were not the normal parties where guests played a few card games while drinking a couple of beers. No, these stags were quite different. Organized and run by the team, they were wild, over-the-edge parties. Players would sell 250–300 tickets in advance, and more people would show up at the door. The stags were right out of Vegas with every imaginable sort of entertainment for men available. Guests were delighted with show girls, dancing, gaming tables, and of course, booze. An amazing number of men would clamour to come to a Rebel stag.

While there were many temptations at the stags, the Rebels had rules. The players did not participate in any of the drinking or frolicking. There was no deviating from the script, as the players knew that a bunch of men surrounded by girls and alcohol was a formula for trouble. The Rebels were very diligent on the controls. They were the bouncers and the peace keepers. The team ran a number of stag fundraisers over the years, yet never once was there an incident or trouble. One thing was for sure: What happened at a Rebel stag, stayed at a Rebel stag.

Everyone had a role in selling tickets, but there were specific stag party assignments, as well. Some would manage the money, some would manage the games, and some would manage the food. Some would set up; others would clean up. Harry personally took care of the entertainment. Everyone, however, was to make sure all the guests had a good time, were kept safe and spent a lot of money.

Keeping things fun and lighthearted was never easy at the stags, but most of the guests were respectful of the Rebels and knew that any nonsense would not be tolerated. The Rebels' tough guys always made their presence noticed. The stags were great successes and fabulous fundraisers for the team. The Rebels had found a formula off the ice to ensure the players didn't have to reach too deep into their own pockets to keep the team going.

The Rebels were a great hockey team and it was important that they looked the part. They didn't want the best team in senior hockey to look like a bunch of scruffy derelicts. The money raised in the stags would pay for league fees and tournaments, but some of it was allocated to uniforms, as well. The Rebels wanted to look like the best team on ice. The initial Rebel logo was the word REBELS in block letters printed on an orange-and-white jersey. After the first year, they changed their colours to red and white, and changed the lettering to script.

In 1972, during the Canada-Russia Summit series, Team Canada sported red-and-white jerseys which had a stylized red leaf. The red leaf rose from the bottom of the jersey looking like the rising sun. Impressed with that look, the Rebels took the half-leaf concept and developed a jersey that had a similar, Canadian feel for the 1973 season. The jerseys were red and white with a diagonal half leaf. The word REBELS ran along the side of the half leaf. That jersey became the symbol of the Rebels for years to come. Their look was quite different from the other teams, and when the players would put the jersey on for the first time, they would feel something very special.

As time progressed, the Lambton League became an elite league within the Toronto senior hockey league. All teams in the league were high-caliber and well-respected, but the Rebels were the class of the league. Yet they were still not content and wanted to see how they could compete on a bigger stage, one beyond the Lambton League.

CHAPTER 4

FROM GOOD TO GREAT

Canadian rinks were filled every day with boys, girls, men and women who were there because they loved the game and the competition. They were ordinary people having fun, searching for the personal reward of knowing they were the best. Newspapers did not write stories about the players. There were no television interviews, no fame, no fan following and no living the high life.

Back then, there were a number of tournaments where teams could compete against each other for bragging rights as the top team in a province. In minor hockey circles, tournaments were very well organized and were sanctioned events, but in the senior circles, the tournaments were organized as fundraisers, generally in small towns. There was a world of hockey outside the pros where players would come together to compete for fun and pride. Through word of mouth and reputation, teams would know what the competition would be like. The players were not paid to play. They all had jobs or attended schools. The competition at all levels was intense and competitive.

The Rebels had made a name for themselves as one of the best senior hockey teams in Ontario and participated in a number of these tournaments. The classic tournament, and the one that distinguished the Rebels outside the Lambton League, was the Way-Jay tournament held in Kitchener, Ontario. Way-Jay was a radio station that sponsored a number of elimination tournaments, that culminated in grand championship. It attracted teams from Toronto to the Kitchener area. Kitchener was a hot bed of hockey having both a Junior A team, (the Kitchener Rangers) as well as a Senior A team, (the Galt Hornets). Both teams were well-established icons. The Hornets had won the Allan Cup (the trophy awarded annually to the national Senior A men's ice hockey champions of Canada) in the 1968-69 season. Although considered amateur, Sr A players were paid to play. To stay competitive in the Senior A league, the Hornets tried to keep players between the ages of 21 and 25. The next stop for many of the players who left the Hornets was the senior team in Cambridge. Consequently, Cambridge was always a very good team and was a powerhouse in the senior circuit.

The reputation of the Rebels had spread, and Cambridge, which was a stronger, more experienced team, during the upcoming Way-Jay tournament, wanted to show the upstarts who the kings of senior hockey were. Most their players had played Senior A for Galt, and a few went as far as semi-pro. Cambridge had not lost a game in any tournament in which it had competed during the past two seasons. Although it was not a formal title, Cambridge was the Ontario Senior champions. Both the Cambridge team and the Rebels had won preliminary tournaments to qualify for the Championship one.

The Championship had two divisions. The organizers put Cambridge in one division and the Rebels in another, hoping that if things went the way they should, the two top teams would meet for the championship game. Sure enough, both Cambridge and the Rebels won their divisions, and a classic confrontation was set. The play of both teams was scrutinized throughout the tournament, and while the chatter suggested it would be a good game, it put Cambridge as having the edge.

Much was on the line, and once the game finally started, Cambridge wasted no time and quickly took a 2–0 lead. It appeared it was going to be a rout for the veteran team.

As the game progressed, Doug Handy, the Rebels goaltender, shouldered the team on his back and made several miraculous saves. Without him the score would have been much worse. The game was tough and hard fought but extremely clean, which was unexpected in this type of hockey. The Cambridge team was on a mission, and they stuck to good, solid, hard-nosed, penalty-free hockey. They pushed the pace of the play, seeming to catch the Rebels off guard, who were not used to being under this kind of pressure.

Eventually, the Rebels got the jitters out of their system, and they started to play their game. By the middle of the second period, the score was tied 2–2. John Collins, a first-year player with the Rebels, had scored both Rebel goals, and then scored his third—a natural hat trick—as the teams exchanged goals to end the period 3–3.

After the second intermission, both teams came out flying with the Rebels taking the lead early. In team sports, the whole team needs to contribute and be their best at all times to win. But there are always certain players who, in various situations, seem to jump to the front of the line and take the leadership role. This was the case with John Collins during this game, who hit the back of the net for the fourth time during the third period. He was no stranger to pressure in hockey, having played minor hockey in the Etobicoke, and eventually junior hockey with the North York Rangers. John was offered a scholarship in the U.S. but broke his ankle prior to the start of the season. The break ended his scholarship hopes.

John could have been Wayne Gretzky's double. Not only did he look like "The Great One," but he played the same, as well. Like Gretzky, John could anticipate the play and place himself where the puck was going to be. He was always one step ahead. His day job was serving as the vice president of sales for Bauer skates, equipping all the NHL teams with skates and managing all the endorsements. He was no stranger to hockey teams and big-name players, and would occasionally tease the other Rebels players by telling them which pros he scrimmaged with each week. Not only was he a great player, but he was an ambassador of the game as well.

The Rebels' lead was short-lived as Cambridge tied it up quickly after John's fourth goal. The game went end-to-end and the pace was unbelievable. Neither team would relent. Back and forth, up and down, both teams had good scoring chances much to the delight of the packed arena. The much-anticipated showdown between the two teams was not a disappointment. This was Senior hockey at its best. With about five minutes left to play, John ignited the Rebels again, scoring his fifth goal to put the Rebels up 5–4. His performance was unbelievable! Cambridge pressed hard, but Handy was a brick wall in the net, making save after save.

As Cambridge pressured, the Rebels sprung Rick Osbourne, a winger, on a breakaway pass. He raced up the ice. (It was ironic that Osbourne would be in the position of winning the game, because a few years later, he would become the coach of the Kitchener University women's hockey team and would be a Cambridge-Kitchener advocate and fan.) He had a wicked wrist shot, and the Rebels knew he would shoot for the top corner of the net, which appeared open. The puck came off his stick like it had been fired from a cannon, heading for the top stick-side of the goal. The Cambridge net minder made a fabulous blocker save, however, and the game continued.

With less than a minute to play, the Cambridge goalie rushed to the bench to give the team an extra attacker. Bob Sidey, former star of the University of Toronto, anchored the Rebels' defence. He logged a huge amount of ice time in the third period and was policing the Rebels' end of the rink where the puck was buzzing around. Time seemed to stand still. The crowd was going crazy and the noise was deafening. Cambridge fired a shot from the point, but Doug kicked it out. Standing at the side of the net, uncovered, stood the extra Cambridge player. The rebound bounced directly on his stick. Doug was down and Bob dove to stop the shot. The puck hit him but deflected over the right shoulder of the sprawling Rebel goalie and into the net. The game was tied 5–5! This competition would have to be settled in overtime.

Overtime started the way the third period had ended. Both teams established a vicious pace from the moment the puck dropped. The Cambridge bench was loudly encouraging each other: "They are a bunch of kids, c'mon let's show them!"

The Rebels' bench was equally as loud and encouraging: "We've got them on the ropes, they're tiring, let them have it!"

Just then a Cambridge player got a break and was streaking up the wing. The Falcon knew the Cambridge player was going to try to cut to the centre from the wing for a direct shot on net. He put on a burst of speed and struck the Cambridge player with a thunderous body check. Both players crashed into the boards and went down heavily. The game stopped as both players had to be helped off the ice. The others caught their breaths during the short delay. Now each team was short a player.

The game continued back and forth with both goalies making excellent saves. After 10 minutes of overtime, the competition remained tied.

A second overtime ensued. Cambridge was tiring, so the Rebels had a distinct edge. They took control of the play changing their lines quickly and keeping the pressure on. The adrenaline was flowing.

Now it was the Cambridge goalie's turn to be unbeatable. He made nothing short of brilliant saves. John Collins, who was looking for a double hat trick, broke through centre ice and was fed a beautiful breakaway pass by John Good with 1:30

left in the period. Collins drove to the goal. He faked a shot to the glove side and shifted to the left. The goalie went down and Collins backhanded it to the top shelf. It appeared that the game was going to be over, but the puck hit the crossbar and went over the glass. Cambridge was still alive.

The second overtime also ended in a tie. At this point, no one knew what was going to take place; ending in a tie after double-overtime had not been anticipated. Eventually the tournament organizers decided that the game would end through a shootout. Each team would have five shots, and the team with most goals would be the winner. Back then, shootouts were only used in Europe and the Olympics. This was no way to settle a great game, but it needed to end somehow.

During the shootout, both goalies were sensational. After each team took four shots, the game remained tied as no one had scored. They were now down to one remaining shot each. Cambridge had saved its top shooter until the end. He came in quickly and fired a slap shot at the top corner of the net. Although the shot had "goal" written all over it, Doug acrobatically threw out his glove to make another spectacular save.

Now it was the Rebels' turn. The team had already used its sniper, John Collins, earlier in the shootout, and he had been robbed by the Cambridge goalie. Johnny Good was the final shooter for the Rebels. He was one of the team's most prolific scorers and was a phenomenal athlete, having excelled in both hockey and baseball where he was a star second baseman for the Toronto Maple Leafs, a high-level minor league baseball club. Jack Domenico, the president of the baseball Maple Leafs, used to describe him as a vacuum cleaner on second base, as no ball would get by him. Good was a cerebral hockey player, a student of the game. He would study the opposing players to see where their strengths and weaknesses were, and he remembered that his teammate John Collins had the breakaway near the end of regulation time and had hit the crossbar nearly scoring on a deke. Most of the Rebels' shooters in the shootout had also tried to deke with no success. Good streaked in from the left, giving the appearance that he, too, was going to shoot. When he reached the goal he decided to deke......

Winning this game, even in a shootout, would change the Rebels' future forever. It wasn't that this would be a decisive win, because after a double overtime and nine shooters, it would be difficult to say that one team was better than the other. For the Rebels, however, winning this game would put the team at the top of the senior hockey league. Beating Cambridge was not the point, but competing with them on an even footing and pushing them to their limits would ensure the Rebels a definite distinction. A win against Cambridge at the Way-Jay tournament would be a foundation for greatness that the Rebels would carry forever. A win would prove to all that this team was very different from the average senior league hockey team.

The puck went into the top corner of the net! Game over! The Rebels won, and their world changed.

Rebels Hockey Team in 1972
Top L-R: Rick McArthur, Wayne Magee, Harry Mellon, Steve Taylor, John Cottrell, Joe Pfaff, Bob Falconi
Bottom L-R: Brian Smith, John Good, Glen Patterson, Tom Bolko, Barry Robb

CHAPTER 5

THE ZANY REBELS

By winning the Way-Jay tournament, the Rebels became Ontario's recognized top team in senior hockey. Their reputation preceded them everywhere they played, and now everyone wanted a piece of them. Although others respected them for what they had attained, the others wanted to prove they were better than the best. As the saying goes, "It is tough to get to the top, but even tougher to stay there." When you are at the top, teams are always trying to knock you off. Every Rebels game was packed with pressure, and they were extremely competitive. The players put great amounts of pressure on themselves, as staying at the top meant you had to keep winning. Not everyone in sports knows how to win. When expectations are low, they can always be met, but when expectations are high, the pressure to meet them can be daunting.

There is always pressure to win when you compete, regardless of the level. It is not just in the pros. While being paid to play has its own issues, such as fans and the media, everyone who takes themselves seriously and competes on any stage has pressure to perform. Learning to continually win and handle the pressure is an art that many individuals and organizations don't know how to do. Vince Lombardi, the legendary coach of the Green Bay Packers in the 1960s, who led his team to three straight Super Bowl victories and five Super Bowls in seven years, said it best in one of his famous quotations: "Winning is not a sometime thing; it's an all the time thing. You don't win once in a while; you don't do things right once in a while; you do them right all of the time."

Winning is a way of life that requires discipline, dedication and passion for excellence. Most athletes, pro or amateur, want—or rather, need—to win. Setting goals, meeting them and overcoming challenges are the keys that drive winners. Handling the pressure of winning and being able to continually perform at a peak level are not traits that come naturally, however. Winning consistently and achieving peak performance has to be learned and continually practiced.

In his book "Outliers: The Story of Success," Malcolm Gladwell contends that achievement is a function of innate talent and preparation. He also contends, however, that as psychologists analyzed the careers of the gifted, they found that preparation played a bigger role than just talent. There are countless examples of players and teams that go from success in one year to failure the next. The Chicago Bulls, New York Yankees, Boston Bruins and Toronto Blue Jays are all teams that have, at times, gone from the top rung of the ladder one year to the bottom rung the next. Causes of success-to-failure could be change of personnel or management philosophy, injuries or something else, but it happens.

This occurs regularly in amateur team sports, too, which is why recreational hockey teams only last an average of three years. Most of the time a team is formed, achieves a certain level of competence, then takes a downward spiral and eventually folds. The declines not only happens with teams, but to individuals, as well. This was the case with Derek Sanderson. For many reasons, some beyond comprehension, he could not maintain his life at the top of his game and quickly descended to the bottom. In life some never win, while for others, winning is a sometime thing.

When the Rebels beat Cambridge in the Way-Jay tournament, even though the margin of victory was minuscule, the pressure to win became even more pronounced. They were the team to beat. In every game they played, the other team had something to prove: They wanted to beat the best. Some thought that it was their right to jump to the top of the ladder and take a shot at being the best with all gain, no pain.

The Rebels knew they had to commit themselves to winning as a way of life or their stay on top would be short-lived. Committing to winning was not a passive action, but rather a conscious decision. They all knew they had created something special. They all knew they had made it to the top. What distinguishes greatness from ordinary is the path you take after the ascent. You either fall down the mountain you just climbed, or you look for the next peak to ascend.

For the Rebels, the win over Cambridge was not a completion but more like the beginning of a new journey. Winning continued to be their way of life, their philosophy. All the players on the team had "real" jobs, of course, and hockey was a hobby. When winning becomes a way of life, it carries into the daily routine, too. The winning didn't stop when the players took off their skates; they all were successful in their personal lives, too.

One of the formulas for the Rebels' continued success was to keep things fun. There had to be a balance between serious hockey and fun. Harry was the guy who ensured that there would be a lot of fun. The word attached to the Rebels' fun times was "zany." They were a bunch of weekend warriors who stretched the limits but had a lot of zany fun together, on and off the ice.

After they won the Way-Jay tournament, the Rebels received many invitations from other teams and tournaments. Everyone wanted a chance to play them. The pressure was on. They could have refused to play and just coast a bit, but Harry and Rick thought it best to get the team right back into the action.

There was a tournament in Leamington, Ontario, that looked like it would be challenging but still a fun one in which to play. It was a well-organized event with teams from all around southwest Ontario, which typically produced a number of very good hockey players and solid teams.

Southwest Ontario always disliked the big city of Toronto, and whenever teams from the Toronto area competed in smaller towns, they were generally at a disadvantage. The refereeing was usually biased, and the smaller town teams would load up with "all-star" players from the area. Leamington was no different. There were a couple of all-star teams, one from St. Thomas and one from London that were waiting for a chance to play the "hot shot" Rebels.

At the beginning of the tournament, the games were fairly relaxed and easy. It changed that Saturday, however.

Saturday featured the tournament's highlight game: the Rebels against St. Thomas. After the highlight game was the town's annual, massive pasta party, which was supported by over 700 local families who came to enjoy the game and the festivities. The following day would be the championship game.

The Rebels and St. Thomas had made it to the championship game on Sunday, no matter who won Saturday's contest, so while the highlight game meant nothing to the outcome of the tournament, pride was on the line, but even more importantly, it would set a precedent for the following day's championship game.

It was an ambush in the making, however.

St. Thomas was a good team that didn't need any help to win, but the refereeing was quite biased. The Rebels could not get out of the penalty box. St. Thomas would hack and commit all kinds of infractions without punishment. When the Rebels retaliated, they would be penalized. The Rebels were trounced soundly 6–2 in that game, much to the delight of the St. Thomas players and fans who came to see the big city Rebels get beaten.

At the end of the game, Harry could see the disappointment on the players' faces. It looked like a no-win situation on Sunday. In the history of the Rebels, very few times had they felt dejection, but this was certainly one of them. The tension in the dressing room could be cut with a knife. The players voiced many complaints about the referees and how the St. Thomas team enjoyed the benefit of one-sided calls. The odds were clearly stacked against them for the next day. They didn't mind losing to a good team, as long as the playing field was level. But it obviously was not the case in Leamington. Harry knew he would have to take charge and change the mood.

After everyone had showered and were ready to leave the dressing room, Harry insisted that they attend the town pasta party. This was the biggest event in this town all year, and the Rebels had to support it. Most of the players protested, but Harry would not take no for an answer. "Boys, show up at the pasta party. You won't be disappointed."

When crazy Harry said something like that, you knew he had a trick or two up his sleeve, and you didn't want to miss the excitement.

Streaking was popular back in those days. Unlike today, where at large sporting events fans have to go through metal detectors for fear that someone has a weapon, back in the mid-1970s, the most stadiums had to worry about was someone running on the field or court naked.

Harry had a history of such behaviour.

After the Rebels had won their first championship in the Lambton League, the team stayed in the locker room for a couple of hours, enjoying some beers and celebrations. As they were gathering to leave, they could hear another game going on in the arena. More than 3,000 people were enjoying a Pee Wee (12-year-olds) game between teams from Ontario and Newfoundland. Harry had just stepped out of the shower and decided to lace up his skates—stark naked! He grabbed a goalie mask and a hockey stick and started walking down the corridor toward the ice.

As the referee dropped the puck to start the second period, Harry jumped over the boards, stole the puck, skated toward one of the goalies and took a shot on net. The fathers in the stands were laughing while the mothers were covering their toddlers' eyes. The referees were blowing their whistles and chasing Harry around the ice. What a commotion! Based on this event, the next year the Lambton senior league was the only one in Canada with a condition that read "ANY PLAYER CAUGHT STREAKING WOULD RECEIVE A YEAR SUSPENSION."

The Leamington pasta party was immense with 1,500 people attending it. The Rebels had thought that this was just another regular tournament. They had no idea how important it was to this small town in southwest Ontario. No wonder there was a push to have a local team win!

Everyone was there, including the other hockey teams, representatives from the police and fire departments, and, of course, the local politicians. Grace before the meal was said by the community's Catholic priest, who blessed the food and wished the players safety and good health throughout the tournament. The Mayor was not feeling well, so his wife gave the opening address. She spoke from the stage in the magnificently decorated hall. NHL games did not have this kind of pomp and ceremony. It was a perfect setting for one of Harry's stunts.

Harry was nowhere to be found. Two other players, Texan (Wayne Magee) and a new recruit named Lawrence, strangely were not there either.

It was a great party. The Rebels put the loss behind them and were enjoying the pasta meal. Noise, commotion and fun abounded. People had to line up buffet style to get their pasta, and the lines were tremendous.

Just then Harry showed up at the Rebels' table. He noticed Rick had already received his food, so he went up to him and stuck his hand in his plate and helped himself to some of his pasta. Rick, never to be thrown off by Harry, continued eating as though nothing happened, but Harry had a mischievous look in his eyes. He soon disappeared into the crowd, and the players went back to enjoying their dinners.

About 30 minutes later, after everyone was seated comfortably and started to have dessert, the lights in the hall dimmed. A voice that sounded a lot like Harry's came over the loudspeakers and said, "Ladies and gentlemen, please turn your attention to the front stage where we will have a performance by the one and only Hanson brothers!"

In 1977, one of the most famous hockey movies of all time, "Slap Shot," starring Paul Newman, was released. The film depicted the crazy world of semi-pro hockey based on a fictional team, the Charlestown Chiefs. The Chiefs were a dismal team until the fighting Hanson brothers joined them. The movie followed the team's ascension once they acquired the rough-and-tumble siblings, who fought their way into popularity and fame. The brother's trademark was their thick-lensed, black-framed glasses with white hockey tape on the nose bridge.

Although the movie was fictional, there were many truths in it about hockey at the semi-pro level in the 1970s. "Slap Shot" portrayed semi-pro hockey as a gong show of goons, fighting each other to the delight of the fans. Even the top NHL teams in the 1970s had a similar makeup. The Boston Bruins were known as the "Big Bad Bruins." The Philadelphia Flyers were nicknamed the "Broad Street Bullies."

While the Hanson brothers were fictional characters, they were based on the Carlson brothers, who were actual hockey players, and two of the brothers actually starred in the film.

So now the town of Leamington was going to be delighted by a visit from the Hansons. What a thrill this would be!

Everyone jumped to their feet as the stage curtain opened. There were shouts and a giant round of applause. Loud disco music boomed through the speakers. On stage appeared Harry, Texan and Lawrence. They were dancing to the music wearing nothing but smiles and black-rimmed glasses with tape on the nose bridge. Reveling in the attention, they danced to the song "Staying Alive." Remarkably, other than a few irate mothers who covered their children's eyes, the crowd roared with laughter. The more Harry, Texan and Lawrence danced, the louder the clapping and whistling became.

As the song came to an end, the mayor's wife ran up to the stage and threw a $10 bill at the dancers. Harry picked up the ten spot, and the three calmly walked off stage to whistles and thunderous applause. Later, when Harry and the crew came back to the Rebels' table, fully clothed, they were swamped by autograph seekers and people with cameras (there were no smart phones then) wanting to take pictures with the Hanson imposters. The rest of the Rebels just shook their heads in disbelief.

It wasn't until sometime later that the players realized that Harry and his dance mates came to the rescue of the Rebels. Harry knew he had to take the pressure off what was a festering powder keg. His antics, though zany, ensured that the Rebels knew that they were special and unique. The pressure of being on top never bothered the Rebels again. They knew that no matter what, there was always light at the end of each tunnel. Harry's antics only went to heighten the reputation of the Rebels and did nothing to deter their popularity. Invites to other tournaments only increased.

The Rebels didn't win the tournament in Leamington. They lost in the championship game 4–2. The refereeing again was questionable, but it didn't matter. As they headed for home, the Rebels held their heads high and walked with swaggers in their strides. They knew going into Leamington that their reputation as a hockey team was established. As they left, they knew their reputation as a zany, crazy, fun-loving bunch of "rebels" was firmly in place. The team was becoming legendary.

The Rebels Hockey Team in 1974
Top L-R: Wayne Magee, Joe Pfaff, Rick Osbourne, John Bostock, Steve Taylor, John Cottrell, Rick McArthur
Bottom L-R: Barry Robb, Bob Falconi, Tom Bolko, Glen Patterson, John Good, Harry Mellon, Brian Smith

CHAPTER 6

FROM SENIOR TO OLD-TIMER HOCKEY

It's hard to believe that a bunch of high school kids, who were brought together to seek revenge on a group of older, cocky and egotistical men, could over time actually change attitudes toward the way senior hockey should be played. But the Rebels, through their abilities and antics, brought a dignity to senior hockey that had not been there before. The Rebels were respected as a great team as well as ambassadors of the game. Over the years, as players and as a team, they continued to bring more respect to the game in a special way.

In Canada, hockey is a team sport that can be played for many years. There are players 70 years old and older who continue to play. It's the same rink, the same rules and the same competitiveness—it's just at a slower pace. The problem with aging hockey players is that most become more interested in the chicken wings and beer after the games and less about the hockey itself. Many let themselves get out of shape, so the quality of play deteriorates.

That was not the case with the Rebels. As the players aged, they continued to keep their competitive edge and worked at being a dominant force in the leagues and tournaments in which they played. Wherever they laced up, they brought their well-earned reputation with them. What's more, the team kept evolving over time. Although there were many Type A personalities on the team, the good of the team was always foremost on everyone's mind. The players checked their egos at the dressing room door, knowing the whole was greater than the sum of the parts. The players fed off that and knew that just being on the team made them better.

As time marched on, the team would continue to evolve, and slight changes and modifications were made, as one player would leave and another would join. To be a part of the team, you had to buy into its culture and rules. The value system was very clear for any who joined: play to win; camaraderie; the team is more important than the individuals; and respect for teammates and the opposition. The Rebels continued holding these values, and they were the dominant fixture in senior hockey in Ontario. They played, they had fun, and they continued to win. Their formula for success was unrivalled.

In the hockey world, you are considered an "old-timer" at age 35. Old-timer teams are abundant and have many tournaments in which they can play, but because of the demand for arena ice time, old-timer leagues are not quite as abundant as those for younger players.

By 1986, most of the Rebels had reached 35 years of age and were looking forward to playing in the old-timer leagues. The team had existed for 17 years, and old-timer hockey was a natural progression. They still wanted to compete at a serious hockey level, but didn't want to have to play against those who were 10 to 15 years younger.

Some old-timer leagues included ex-pros who joined good leagues after their pro careers ended. The result was numerous recreational hockey teams that continued to play the game, and some exceptionally good leagues that had top-quality and competitive old-timer teams existed.

One such league was the old-timer league at George Bell Arena in Toronto. This league had some of the best teams in Ontario, such as the Italian old-timers, Panasonic and Kanes Chevy. The league had been operating for about eight years and had attracted some of the best players 35 and older in the area. When the league had an opening for a team, the Rebels jumped at the chance to join.

The Rebels entry into the George Bell, which was an extremely competitive old-timer league, was not easy. The reputation the Rebels had built as a tough, hard-nosed team was disturbing to many playing old-timer hockey. "These guys take it too seriously," "They are too rough," and "They are a dirty team," were some of the attitudes the Rebels faced. The ambassadors of the senior game had become the villains in old-timer leagues. The red carpet was not rolled out for them. The Rebels were a good team, but it was not as though they were going to go into the old-timer leagues, particularly the George Bell League, and blow teams away.

The word "old-timer" implies a bunch of old guys skating at a snail's pace and having fun. Many leagues were like that, but not this one. This was a league that had excellent players who had played in the pros, Senior A, Junior A and the university level. The teams were very protective of their league and were always nervous about letting new teams into it. The Rebels had to push hard for acceptance. Fortunately, there were enough players on league teams who had played against the Rebels in the past and knew that they would be a good addition to the league.

Eventually, after much pleading and bargaining, the Rebels were accepted into the George Bell League. The addition made this league the absolute best old-timer league in Ontario. Even some of the Rebels felt they could no longer compete at this level and left the team. While some left, others were recruited to join. Although the transition was gradual, it was nonetheless a transformation of the team as it entered the old-timer era. Even though some players stopped playing, they never left the Rebels and would still go to games as loyal fans, supporting the new players and ensuring Rebels' traditions were being followed.

The Rebels team with players age 35 and older had all the same qualities of the team in its younger years. Player changes and additions ensured that the old-timer team would be as strong and as competitive, supporting the same values.

Steve Mauthe, an excellent athlete and a hard-nosed, rock-solid star hockey player who had played Junior A hockey in St. Catharines, Ontario, and had been part of the Minnesota North Star system, was one of the first new recruits. Don Kinsman who had played against the Rebels in the Lambton league was recruited by the team. Don was smooth skating winger who played Junior A in Charlottetown, Prince Edward Island before going to the University of New Brunswick and playing there for three years. Mike Burkart, a rugged defenseman who had played hockey on a scholarship at the University New Hampshire in the U.S., was next to join.

Ottawa was another hockey hotbed that produced many good players. Adrien Pilon, who played in the Ottawa and Montreal area, also became a Rebel. Adrien was a fast, tough, hard-nosed, versatile player who could play forward or defence.

Next getting fitted for a Rebels sweater was Rod Farmer, a tough and determined winger who played his minor hockey with the Don Mills Flyers and went to York University as a standout football and hockey player for the Yeomen.

Joining the team as well were Tim Hauun, Mike Hubert and John Bellis. A top-scoring forward for York University, Tim added speed and tenacity to the Rebels' forward lines. Greg, who had played his minor hockey in the Metro Toronto Hockey League, was a swift-skating winger and an adept scorer. John, a selfless, all-star goalie who had played for numerous senior teams, would share goaltending duties with Doug Handy. John had a great sense of humour and would keep the team loose. When a puck got by him, his favourite line was, "The puck didn't go where he shot it!"

Other welcome additions to the team were Bruce Wells, Ron Wynne and Dave Cobban. A two-way player who graduated from Kent State where he also played on a hockey scholarship, Wells added great drive and flair to the team as well as leadership in the dressing room. Ron, an all-star player at Ryerson University, was perhaps one of the most talented players on the team. Dave, a standout at the University of Guelph, was another Wayne Gretzky-type player: a very smooth-skating playmaker and sniper. Not only did he lead the team in scoring for years, but he and Ron took on the management of the Rebels when they started playing in the old-timer leagues. In the history of the Rebels, Dave was considered the best all-round player ever to put on the Rebels jersey. He embodied all the traits that defined the Rebels.

With the new players added to the core nucleus of the Rebels, once again they were a powerhouse, only this time it was in a new league.

The other teams in the league knew every game against the Rebels was going to be tough. Although the league eventually embraced the Rebels because they brought even more credibility to an already good league, the teams themselves would not give an inch to the new team. Each game was a battle.

All old-timer leagues try to keep the rough stuff to a minimum with zero tolerance for fighting. In hockey, fighting was always a deterrent for those who were liberal with their sticks. Stick infractions, such as high-sticking, slashing or spearing, usually ended up with the recipient dropping the gloves and swinging. Most of the players grew up with those unwritten rules of the game, which usually kept stick infractions to a minimum.

Yet in old-timer play, with fighting entirely out of the game, stick infractions were the norm. Even the little guys would act big with a stick in their hands. The Rebels found out early that they would have to adjust their attitude. As the new team in the league, the Rebels were on the receiving end of many cheap stick shots by some not-so-worthy opponents— unworthy in the sense that if the rules weren't what they were, fewer liberties would have been taken. High sticks welcomed the

Rebels into the new league, but this was nothing new for them. The Rebels knew the secret was to just keep playing hard and to not back down as they had enough talent and toughness to play any style of game.

The top two teams in the league were not about to be pushed out of their spots by the new team—not without a battle, anyway. First came the Italians. They were a very well-respected team that played in many tournaments and had numerous players who had played pro and semi-pro hockey. Leading them was Norm Ullman, a former Toronto Maple Leaf and Detroit Red Wing who is a proud member of the Hockey Hall of Fame. Ullman may have been aging, but he still was one of the best players on the ice with amazing skills.

The Italian team also had Mike Pelyk, a former Toronto Maple Leaf, and Bob Lorimer, who had played for the New York Islanders. They joined a number of seasoned veterans, most of whom had played semi-pro hockey in their younger years.

The game was fast-paced from the beginning to end. The Italians were a classy team and stuck to playing hockey without much rough stuff. The competition featured some excellent play making, and the ex-pros were interesting to play against.

Early in the game, the Italians seemed to take it easy and go through the motions, but as the game progressed, they saw that the Rebels were playing their hearts out and presented stiff competition. The Italians elevated their game and put it into another gear, but the Rebels would not to be overwhelmed or intimidated. The battle ended with the Rebels winning 5–3.

Next came Panasonic. It was an interesting team. It had some excellent players, such as Paddy Keenan, Peter Noakes, Don Amos and Howard Hampton, who all had played in junior or semi-pro leagues in their youth.

Panasonic also had Dave Trudel, a feisty, tough winger who honed his skills playing junior A hockey in Ottawa. (After playing a few years with Panasonic, he joined the Rebels.) They also had the meanest and toughest guy by far in the league, John (Mack Truck) MacKenzie. He was a retail executive by day but a powerhouse hockey player at night.

The makeup of the Panasonic team was interesting because many of the players had executive jobs and travelled frequently. As such, they had problems icing a full team in all games. With a full team, they were as good as anybody in the league.

When they were short-handed, they could hold their own for the first two periods, but then they tired in the third.

The first game against the Rebels they had a short bench. The game was tied at the end of the second period 2–2. In the third, however, the Rebels took over, and the game ended 5–2.

Then came Kanes Chevy, which was sponsored by a local GM dealer. It was a very strong and competitive team, as well. Like the Italians, it was well-known in the old-timer circles. It had a few ex-pros, such as former Toronto Maple Leaf Terry Clancy, and was stacked with former University of Toronto alumni who had won many Ontario and National University Championships. A skilled, fast team that liked to play tough, Kanes had been the league winners for the previous two years. The Rebels may have surprised the Italians, but the Kanes team was going to be prepared.

As expected, the game started out quite rough and filled with penalties. If Kanes thought they were going to push the Rebels around, they were in for a surprise. The heavy-weights for the Rebels, Steve Mauthe, Steve Taylor and Mike Hubert, started the first shift, and before long there were six people in the penalty box: three from the Rebels and three from Kanes. With only three skaters for each side, there was plenty of skating room.

Dave Cobban went on an end-to-end rush to start the scoring: 1–0 Rebels. Kanes was in a dilemma. They weren't going to intimidate the Rebels, who still had more heavy-weights on the bench in addition to the ones in the penalty box. If they ran into too many penalties, the Rebels would fill their net. Kanes' original strategy was not working. Except for the first shift, which was a penalty fest, the next two periods were chippy and rough but penalty free.

Just prior to the end of the second period, Mike Hubert combined on a great passing play from Steve Mauthe to make it 2–0 Rebels.

Kanes put pressure on in the first five minutes of the third period, but Handy was a stalwart in the net. As time was running out, the rough stuff started again, and the Rebels went toe-to-toe with Kanes, resulting in a parade to the penalty box again.

The game ended with the Rebels winning 2–0. The victory was more than a win on the scoreboard. This was, once again, another statement victory for the team.

This time it was in the old-timer league. Kanes threw everything it could at them, including rough stuff, but the Rebels won the battles on the ice and the scoreboard. Everyone in the league knew that after the Rebels beat the Italians and Panasonic, and now with a convincing win over Kanes, that there would be a changing of the guard.

The winning continued, and the Rebels ended up in first place in the league. They didn't win every game, but they established themselves securely at the top of the league. Every game put them to the test, as they were the team to beat. Eventually the team won its first of many league championships.

The George Bell League was the best old-timer hockey league in Ontario. Every Wednesday night in winter, great, competitive hockey games were played. Players battled each other with superb skill and sportsmanship, playing the game they loved.

Unfortunately, ice time was now at a premium. With the growth of woman's hockey as well as youth hockey, prime ice time became scarce all around Toronto. The major force of minor hockey, the Greater Toronto Hockey League, decided to take prime ice time away from men's leagues and give it to the youth leagues. The men didn't like it, but no one would argue for men to play instead of kids.

The Rebels played in the league five years before the George Bell League folded, leaving some of the best old-timer teams in Ontario without a place to play.

The Rebels and a couple of the George Bell teams moved to a league in Etobicoke. The league called itself an old-timer league, but the rules were rather loose about the definition of old-timer. The Rebels had players between 35 and 45 years of age, but some of the teams had players much younger.

The league played out of the Etobicoke Ice Sports Arena, and the quality of hockey was good. The Rebels played there for a number of years. Teams constantly were changing as the league continued letting in younger players. The Rebels knew that this was not going to work out well for them in the long run. They had to find a way to keep what they had built going. Once again, the Rebels found themselves against a familiar opponent, but it wasn't another team: they needed to find a league that would accept them. Their age classified them as old-timers, but their level of play made them unwelcome in most established, old-timer leagues.

Playing in younger-aged leagues against 20-year-olds was no longer an option, either. The young guys would not appreciate being beaten by "old men," and the old guys would not want to give an inch to the younger players. Playing in a younger league was a formula for injury and problems. Of all the challenges and obstacles the Rebels faced over many years, finding a league to play in was always one of the toughest ones.

Rebels Hockey Team in 1990
Top L-R Barry Robb, John T, George Anderson, Bob Falconi,
Don Kinsman, Bruce Wells, Dave Cobban, Steve Mauthe, Joe Pfaff
Bottom L-R: Brian Smith, Ron Wynne, Doug Handy, John Good, Rod Farmer, Ernie Campe

CHAPTER 7

REBELS 35TH ANNIVERSARY

The Rebels did a lot of research and found a well-established, old-timer league in Mississauga called the Erin Mills League. It had been running for a number of years. While the quality of hockey was average, the league was well-managed and had specific guidelines about the kind of players allowed to participate—the league didn't want any rough stuff. The irony was that some of its current players were the toughest ones around in their younger days, such as Bobby Smith. Many of the Rebels knew Smith from the Lambton League. An all-round athlete, he mastered hockey, football and fastball. He had a tryout with the Argos when they were a powerhouse in the Canadian Football League, and he had played on their taxi squads as he tried to make the big team. In the winter he played hockey in the Lambton League, but not with the Rebels.

The Rebels and Smith had great respect for each other. In the Lambton League, Smith played on a weaker team, but he was his team's leader and competed very hard. He loved playing against the Rebels and getting under their skin. The Rebels loved the challenge he presented. Smith was one of the toughest and most determined hockey players in the league. He was built like a rock with hammer-like hands, and everyone knew not to mess with him. The few players in the league who challenged him always ended up looking like they had gone through a meat grinder. He was given a lot of space.

Not only was Smith a great athlete, but he was a classy individual. He made everyone around him better. Smith was perfect Rebels material, but no matter how hard the players tried, Smith would never join the team.

In any event, with guys like Smith in the league, the Rebels knew that the Erin Mills League would host some tough, competitive games.

The first year the Rebels applied to join the league, they were denied and told there were no openings. But the Rebels felt that other teams knew about them and did not want that level of competition in the league.

Since time was marching on, the Rebels decided to split into two old-timer teams: one with the younger guys who would continue to play in Etobicoke, and one with the older guys who would play in a less competitive league in Oakville, Ontario. This move allowed everyone who wanted to play to continue at whatever level they felt comfortable. Some even played in both leagues. To fill two teams a few of the "retired" Rebels returned to play as well as adding a few additions to the team. Added were Tom Green, George Anderson and Ron Kerr. Tom was a very popular player with the team and league. Tom was a tall strong winger who patrolled the boards. He played his minor hockey in the Toronto Hockey League and continued to excel in the game. Tom also gave back much of himself as a minor league coach working with kids to help their development in the game.

George Anderson was another great contributor to the game as a coach. One of the elite coaches in the Brampton Minor Hockey League, George coached many teams to championships and great success. There is a long list kids who George helped develop into upstanding individuals as well as quality hockey players. As a player himself, George was well known as a clutch and grab defensive specialist. If you stood in front of the net very long, you would soon feel the end of George's stick.

Ron played minor hockey in Brampton before moving on to junior with Streetsville, Burlington and Oakville, Ontario. He then went on to become a star player at Genesco State University in New York, where he led the Knights for three years.

The Rebels stayed in touch with the Erin Mills League, and the following year, one league team didn't pay its entrance fee because they couldn't get enough players to commit. Therefore, the league had an opening, and the Rebels asked to join. Some of the current teams were reluctant to allow them in, but the Rebels knew some of the league managers and pleaded their case. The Rebels committed to be good guys, pay their bills and abide by all the rules of the league. As usual, they would be ambassadors of the game.

The league allowed the Rebels in, but only the older old-timer Rebels could play. An old-timer league specifying which of the old-timer Rebels could play was bizarre! Nonetheless, the Rebels agreed. The "younger" old-timer team continued to play in Etobicoke, and the older team joined the Erin Mills League. Again, a few players played in both. This worked out well because generally the games did not conflict.

It was an interesting time for the Rebels, as they were winning in both leagues despite obstacles.

In the Etobicoke League, the Rebels were battling teams that continued to bring in younger players to make themselves more competitive. With the "younger" Rebels getting older, the team soon became the oldest one by far, giving up at least 10 years of age on average to the other teams. Despite that, the Rebels won four league championships. But given their age, they could see that league championships would start to elude them.

In the Erin Mills League, the Rebels were not a popular team. Of the league's eight teams, four were very strong and four were very weak. The games between strong teams were always close and competitive, but against the weaker teams, all four of the stronger teams would soundly beat them.

The Rebels clearly were the league's best team. Every year they ended in first place, and they won four straight championships. Players from the better teams enjoyed the competition, and in many cases, knew Rebels players from having played with or against them in their youth.

The weaker teams, however, did not appreciate the Rebels, and the Rebels, unfortunately, became the target of their frustrations.

First, unable to compete at the Rebels' level, the weaker teams would spear, slash and high-stick their way into penalty-filled affairs that ended with lopsided scores in favour of the Rebels.

Then, some players on weaker teams would develop "Rebels flu," as it was humorously called, and not show up for their games. While the flu spread through the weaker teams, the stronger teams, including Bobby Smith's, had too much class and competitive spirit to let that happen. They were appreciative of the competition.

Finally, the weaker teams would continually complain to league management that the Rebels were not good for the league and should be banned from it. League managers, who played on some of the stronger teams, actually liked the Rebels, and they understood what was going on with the weaker teams.

The Erin Mills League's constitution allowed teams to vote teams out, however, and with the "ban the Rebels" chirping getting louder, the handwriting was on the wall, and the Rebels knew it would not be long before they would be voted out. Again there were changes coming for the Rebels, and adjustments would have to be made.

By now, 2004, the Rebels had existed for nearly 35 years. For a non-pro, university, high school or minor hockey league team to survive for that many years was quite an accomplishment! It was common for teams like the Toronto Maple Leafs, the University of Toronto Blues or the Mississauga Braves Hockey Association to exist for decades or even surpass the 100-year mark. A team of guys playing in intermediate, senior or old-timer hockey for that long, however, was unheard of.

The Hockey Hall of Fame was approached to acknowledge the Rebel's accomplishment, but the request was politely declined. The Hall said it would, however, mention the Rebels in the Hometown Hockey Heroes section with teams like Wayne Gretzky's Brantford peewee team, on which he scored 400 goals. They would not recognize players who didn't make it to the big leagues or contribute to hockey in some "builder" status form. The Hall typically does not recognize teams—only individuals. The lack of attention by Hall officials was not a surprise. They, too, were products of the system that focuses on those who bring popularity and notoriety to the professional game. The stars are the ones who make it into the self-perpetuating system. Few want to pay attention to those who play for the love of the game and the rewards that are associated with that love.

The Rebels' achievement was acknowledged, however, by some key people. First, Mark Zwolin of the Toronto Star wrote a full-page article about the Rebels in April of 2005 in celebration of their 35th anniversary. The article was entitled, "Rebels: A hall of a cause." His article pointed out, "They've lost some hair or a step or two, but these old-timers have been playing since 1969. Now these fun-loving greybeards are making a bid to join the Hockey Hall of Fame."

The story went on to say that the Rebels should be inducted in to the Hockey Hall of Fame because of their longevity. "They want to be honoured by the Hockey Hall of Fame. It's not because the Rebels think they're the Edmonton Oilers, although they have won more than forty league championships since first joining an industrial league at Lambton Arena in 1969, but their longevity, combined with their commitment to the game and to each other, make them the embodiment of hockey's best trait. Whatever their other merits, the Rebels make a strong case for themselves based on their durability."

The Rebels received other wonderful accolades on their 35th anniversary, including one from Hazel McCallion, the Mayor of Mississauga. She was proud to take ownership of the team, as well. In tournaments, when the Rebels had to declare what city they were from, they always chose Mississauga, even though their roots were originally in Toronto. Many of the players were also living in Mississauga at the time.

Mayor McCallion wrote in a gracious letter of congratulations: "I would like to congratulate the members of the Mississauga Rebels Hockey Team on the 35th anniversary of the team.

"The Rebels longevity is a testament to the players' dedication and passion for the game. The consistently high calibre of play is evident by the numerous championships the team has won during this period. The team members' love of the game is evident by their contribution to the community with many members acting as coaches and mentors-teaching the youth of today about the great game of hockey and how it is played. The Rebels are model sportsmen for the children and youth, in both Mississauga and Toronto, as they share their passion and knowledge of the game.

"I commend the Rebels for their support of the community by dedicating their time to coaching and to various fundraising initiatives over the years. Congratulations on 35 great years."

The Prime Minister of Canada, Paul Martin, extended his congratulations, too: "I am pleased to extend my warmest greetings to the members of the Rebels Hockey Team on the occasion of its 35th anniversary.

"Over the past 35 years, you have invested your time and energy in the enjoyment of hockey. Although each of you has experienced many changes since your high school days, your love of the sport has remained. As you commemorate this special milestone, you will have an excellent opportunity to reflect upon your team's proud history, while also celebrating the ties of friendship and camaraderie that have been the cornerstone of its longevity and success.

"I wish you all a most enjoyable anniversary celebration, as well as every success in the years to come."

To celebrate their accomplishment, the Rebels had a party that included a hockey game in the afternoon in which the players, their sons and daughters played. All those who had ever worn the Rebels sweater were invited, along with their spouses, to a commemorative dinner. George Moore and Dave Montgomery, the referees from the Lambton League, came to honour the Rebels. Mike D'Angelis, who had helped the Rebels for numerous years as manager, came with his wife, Ruth, to celebrate. Mike would show up hours before the game, ensuring the sweaters were hung and the dressing rooms were clean. He managed the game sheets and paid all the bills for the team. He and Ruth loved being around the team and were a tremendous help. They were respected by the Rebels as well as the other teams in the league. Every team wished they had a Mike and Ruth to help them.

Old sweaters and jackets adorned the banquet as well as trophies and pictures. Speeches and tributes were given throughout the night, as fond memories were shared. Of course, the reading of the congratulatory messages from the Mayor of Mississauga and the Prime Minister of Canada were a treat and a surprise for all.

One of the speeches of note, of course, was Harry's. His message was simple: "Never did I realize 35 years ago, when I wanted to set up a team to avenge my punctured lung, did I realize we would be here 35 years later reminiscing and telling tales about our years together. I had no idea that something this great would be created. All I ever wanted to do was beat the crap out of Gary and look what happened."

Joe Pfaff, another one of the team founders, said, "It is a thrill to see everyone gathered here celebrating this wonderful achievement. We put the right players together at the right time and we never looked back. This has been a great journey that is far from over. What a pleasure it has been to be part of this piece of Canadian history."

Perhaps the best lines came from Dave Cobban. Not only was Dave a star player, but he took over the management of the team in the latter years. "Something about putting on the Rebels' jersey, you can sense the heritage, the commitment and the roots. You might come to the rink tired after a long day's work and not feel up to playing, but when you get to the dressing room, look around at the other guys, share in the camaraderie and finally put the jersey on, there is a magic that takes over. The Rebel Magic! You just know you won't be beat," he said.

Rebels 35th Anniversary 2004
Top L-R: Roy Hysen, Danny Hysen, Jeff Bellis, Harry Mellon, George Moore (Referee), Sid Thompson, Joe Pfaff,
Mike Tilley, Tom Green, Rick Robb, Barry Robb, John Cottrell, John Bostock, Steve Taylor, Ron Wynne,
William Cannizzaro, Dave Montgomery (Referee), Tom Butt, Chris Ricci, Gord Kenwood
Bottom L-R: Bob Falconi, Mike Hubert, Don Kinsman, Doug Handy, Rod Farmer, Dave Cobban,
John Good, Bruce Wells, Brian Smith, John Bellis, Mike Burkart, Steve Mauthe, Dave Wregget

BOB FALCONI

FRIDAY, APRIL 22, 2005 • TORONTO STAR • B3

Hockey Through The Ages

The Mississauga Rebels, who have seen their share of dressing rooms in several arenas over the years — they now call the one at Cawthra home — won their old-timers' league championship this season.

Rebels: A hall of a cause

They've lost some hair and a step or two, but these old-timers have been playing shinny since 1969
Now these fun-loving greybeards are making a bid to join the Hockey Hall of Fame, *by Mark Zwolinski*

For more than three decades, Brian Smith's closest friends have been his teammates on the Mississauga Rebels hockey team. They've laughed through weddings and funerals and divorces, cried through funerals and divorces.

But that doesn't mean they're not above giving Smith a hard time about being born without a right hand. The other Rebels call Smith "the clock" — because he's got one long arm and one short arm.

When Smith, who plays with the aid of a prosthetic device, is one-handedly scrubbing his head in the shower after games, a teammate invariably sneaks up from behind, places a hand on the other side of his head and shouts: "Look, it's a miracle!"

Smith and his friends have been a fun-loving group of industrial league players in and around Toronto for more than 35 years. They're now greying over-55s, but these aging Rebels have found a new cause.

They want to be honoured by the Hockey Hall of Fame.

It's not because the Rebels think they're the 1984-88 Edmonton Oilers, although they have won more than 40 league and tournament championships since first joining an industrial league at Lambton Arena in 1969.

But they figure their longevity combined with their commitment to the game and to each other make them the embodiment hockey's best traits.

"We're not looking at ourselves like we're a bunch of heroes or something," says 58-year-old Ron Wynne. "A lot of us guys . . . are coaches now, and we have kids and wives playing the game. I think that's the true measure of hockey success, if your kids and family carry on what you started."

The team has sent letters to the hall of fame asking that they be considered for inclusion. Hall bylaws prohibit enshrining entire teams — including Team Canada 1972 — but it allows temporary displays honouring teams in its museum section.

"We do represent the game at all levels," said hall of fame president Jeff Denomme. "The museum is about telling the stories of hockey, and their (the Rebels') story could enter into recognition as the displays are renewed."

The Rebels would most likely be recognized in the "Hometown Hockey Heroes" section.

The hall is awaiting a team photo to before making a decision and the Rebels posed for one last month after winning their old-timers' league championship.

"I think we have to do a bit more lobbying, too, but we've got our fingers crossed," says Ron Wynne, 54, a right-winger who is considered a Rebel "rookie" with only 20 years' service with the team.

Whatever their other hall of fame merits, the Rebels make a strong case for themselves based just on their durability.

They've moved through industrial and senior leagues at Double Rinks, George Bell Arena and now in Mississauga. In the late 1980s and early 1990s, there were enough players for two teams. The team now plays Wednesday nights at Cawthra Arena.

Through it all, little has changed — except the addition of wrinkles and weight, and the loss of hair and speed. Players have come and gone, but the core group of 12 has stuck together since Richard Nixon was a first-year U.S. president. The Rebels believe there are few

teams that can match that.

"This is everything that's good about hockey," says Wynne. "It's a big family and it exemplifies what the game is about . . . friendships and a positive experience for our children."

Chomping away during a recent wing night at the Clarkson Pump restaurant, the Rebels share laughs while telling tales from their rollicking history. And that history endures in no small part because the players are just about the most important things in each other's lives.

It hasn't mattered where they came from or how much money they earned. Most are hardworking guys who get up early and work late.

Doug Handy owns his own lock business; Bob Falconi is a national marketing manager with Rayovac and is heavily involved in junior hockey with the Oakville Blades; and the Robb brothers — Barry and Rick — have owned and operated a pool business since the late '60s.

Big Joe Pfaff has been an admissions officer at Ryerson University for 32 years and played in the minor leagues for the

Kansas City Royals. Harry Melon defies athletic logic by continuing to play after surviving a brain aneurysm.

Sacrifices have been many. Each player spends roughly $2,500 per year to keep up the hockey habit, meaning the Rebels have gone through well over $1 million in their history.

To a man, though, the Rebels feel it all has been more than worth it. Where else would they get their stories?

In 1995, for instance, former Maple Leaf Wilf Paiement was recruited to join the team by Steve Mauthe, who had played with Paiement in Niagara Falls.

"One of our guys brought in an old Wilf Paiement hockey card because he was really overweight when he played with us," recalls Wynne. "The card said he was six-feet, 190-pounds . . . but someone said in our dressing room, 'When was that, at birth?' "

Ribbing, obviously, is standard Rebel practice. The teammates yell at each other on the ice and on the bench, sometimes with such vigour that other players, even referees, do double takes.

"If you went into the average household, you'd probably see the same thing," Wynne says. "There's a fine line there, and a lot of people think we're nuts. But for us, it's a sign of how close we are."

The Rebels celebrated their 35th anniversary last August with a weekend celebration that attracted more than 60 current and past players.

How much longer the Rebels is unknown. But they show no signs of slowing down.

Falconi still runs marathons. Melon, 58, played middle linebacker in U of T alumni football games until he was 49 when the Blues politely kicked him out because of his age.

Bruce Wells decided he could match Falconi and ran his own marathon — without any training. The only injury he suffered was bleeding nipples.

"I guess I forgot to tell him you had to rub Vaseline on them because your shirt rubs against them so much they bleed," Falconi said, laughing.

"You have to be thick-skinned to play on this team."

Toronto Star Article on April 22, 2005

48

OFFICE OF THE MAYOR

August 19, 2004
Our File: M.02.08

Mr. Bob Falconi
Divisional Manager - Canada
Rayovac Canada Inc.
5448 Timberlea Road
Mississauga, Ontario
L4W 2T7

Dear Mr. Falconi:

I would like to congratulate you and the other members of the Mississauga Rebels Hockey Team on the 35th anniversary of the team.

The Rebels' longevity is a testament to the players' dedication and passion for the game. The consistently high calibre of play is evident by the numerous championships the team has won during this period.

The team members' love of the game is evident by their contribution to the community with many members acting as coaches and mentors - teaching the youth of today about the great game of hockey and how it is played. The Rebels are model sportsmen for children and youth, in both Mississauga and Toronto, as they share their passion and knowledge of the game.

I commend the Rebels for their support of the community by dedicating their time to coaching and to various fundraising initiatives over the years.

Congratulations on 35 great years.

Sincerely,

HAZEL McCALLION
MAYOR

THE CORPORATION OF THE CITY OF MISSISSAUGA
300 CITY CENTRE DRIVE, MISSISSAUGA, ONTARIO L5B 3C1
TEL: 905-896-5555   FAX: 905-896-5879
mayor@city.mississauga.on.ca

Mayor Hazel McCallion's Congratulatory Letter to the Rebels in 2004

PRIME MINISTER · PREMIER MINISTRE

I am pleased to extend my warmest greetings to the members of the Mississauga Rebels Hockey Team on the occasion of its 35th anniversary.

Over the past 35 years, you have invested your time and energy in the enjoyment of hockey. Although each of you has experienced many changes since your high school days, your love of the sport has always remained. As you commemorate this special milestone, you will have an excellent opportunity to reflect upon your team's proud history, while also celebrating the ties of friendship and camaraderie that have been the cornerstone of its longevity and success.

I wish you all a most enjoyable anniversary celebration, as well as every success in the years to come.

OTTAWA
2004

Prime Minister Paul Martin's Congratulatory Letter to the Rebels in 2004

Back in the Etobicoke and Erin Mills Leagues, the magic continued with both teams excelling. The younger Rebels in the Etobicoke league made it to the championship round while the older Rebels in the Erin Mills league won the championship again.

It was not a surprise a few days after the Erin Mills championship trophy presentation that league representatives told the Rebels that they would not be welcome back to play the next year. The Rebels were disappointed and gave the championship trophy back.

The run at Erin Mills had ended. The weaker teams had cast their votes, and the Rebels were gone. No doubt the better teams in the league were not happy with the decision, either. They probably missed the intense competition, too.

The irony was that many of the Rebel players were later invited to play on various teams in the league. Strange situation indeed!

Soon after that, the Etobicoke League folded as, once again, ice time was allocated to minor hockey leagues.

At this point, the two teams combined to form one team and played out of a league at Lakeshore Arena in Toronto. This was a typical over-35-years-old, old-timer league, so the Rebels were once again the oldest team. A team named the Red Wings had won the league championship two years in a row. When the manager of the Red Wings met Rebels' management at a league meeting, he remarked that he understood that the team had lost very few games in their history. "They better get used to losing in this league," was his final statement. He had no idea whom he was talking about. The Rebels played there from 2006 to 2008 and won three consecutive championships. The league was well-managed, but some of the teams appeared to be financially shaky, which meant that the league would eventually fold.

There was a very good old-timer league at Centennial Arena in Etobicoke that the Rebels wanted to join. The team had tried to join the league the previous year, but was turned down as there was no vacancy. Some of the players in the league were from the George Bell League. They knew the Rebels well and wanted them to join the league to enhance the quality of play. There were teams at the lower-end of the pack, however, who, as usual, were concerned about the Rebels joining.

It appeared that the Rebels were not going to have a league to play in. Plans were being made just to play in tournaments, and some of the older Rebels decided it was time to hang up their skates. Then the Centennial League called. Three games into the season, a league team folded. It had problems getting players, and as such, could not pay its bills. League organizers knew it would be difficult to reschedule games, plus they would have an odd number of teams in the league. They approached the Rebels and said if they were willing to pay the full commitment to the league and accept that they had zero points after three games, they could join the league. Rebels agreed and started playing the next week. That year, 2008, they finished in second place but won the league championship, and thus started a long and happy relationship with the Centennial League.

The league was extremely well-managed with top-notch rules and regulations that were adhered to. The refereeing, too, was superb. Sam Marra, who had refereed the Rebels in the past, was one of the senior officials. There was mutual respect between the Rebels and Marra, and there never were any issues in the league because of Marra's ability to call the right penalties while still allowing the men to play hard.

The Rebels were a welcome addition. Many old rivalries were renewed and new ones were formed. The Rebels constantly were a contending team, always finishing near the top of the pack. They were a team of distinction and assisted in the management of the league as well.

The Rebels played in the Centennial League for seven years. As with all the other leagues, they would see teams come and go. Players would be recycled from one team to another. Often the colour of the jerseys would change along with team names. Some players would play on one team one year, and on another the next. The constant in the league was the Rebels. They would show up in their new sweaters, basically the same group of guys, and would be first to pay the league fees. Every game would be a hard-fought match with great sportsmanship at the end. Even the zaniness continued, led by Harry, of course. His antics were non-stop. Before games, he would visit the referees and the other teams' dressing rooms and inundate them with jokes he had told the Rebels hundreds of times. The others were fresh meat.

Age never seemed to be a big factor for the Rebels. To play in the Centennial League, players had to be over 40 years old. By 2008, most of the Rebels players were in their mid-to-late 50s. Again, in this league, like others they played in, they were the oldest. The other teams knew the Rebels well so they didn't treat them gently because they were older. The Rebels seemed to take a page from American comedian George Burns who said, "You can't help getting older, but you don't have to get old."

Dave Cobban would call it the "Rebel Magic." The other teams would call it a bunch of good old guys who knew how to play and compete. Whatever it was, the Rebels were always in each game and competing to the last whistle. When they were younger, they rarely lost games, however, as they aged in the Centennial League, they had to get used to losing a few now and then…but only a few.

During one championship game, about 15 retired Rebels came out to watch and cheer on the team. During stoppages in play, the opposing team would comment to some of the players on the ice, "You guys are amazing, it just never ends." That was true. The spirit, the camaraderie and the passion never ended for any of the guys who were fortunate enough to the wear the Rebels' jersey.

CHAPTER 8

MORE THAN A GAME

Hockey is one of the few games that is played worldwide. Canadians have always cherished and protected hockey as their own as it has become the country's national sport. Although Canadians claim ownership of the game, evidence shows that a type of stick-and-ball game was played in Egypt in 400 B.C. Ice hockey, as we know it, may have derived from Native Americans who played lacrosse. Many tribes throughout North America played a version of field hockey, which involved some type of "puck" or ball and curved, wooden sticks. Ice hockey was observed by Europeans who saw Mi'kmaq native people in Nova Scotia in the late 17th century play what they called "rickets" or "hurley" with a frozen road apple as a puck.

In 1836, Thomas Chandler Haliburton made a literary reference in one of his writings, "The Clockmaker," to "playing ball on ice," which also describes hurley. When not studying at King's College School in Windsor, Nova Scotia, Haliburton and his friends evidently enjoyed playing the game.

The modern form of ice hockey could be credited to Nova Scotia-born James Creighton, who has been called "The Father or Godfather of Organized Hockey." Others designate him the "Inventor of Hockey." Creighton, however, is quoted as humbly stating, "I had the honour to be captain of the first regular hockey club to be formed in Canada."

Born in 1850, Creighton had seen a stickball game played on ice in Halifax. He fell in love with the game and learned how to play it. Later in life, he moved to Montreal to study law at McGill University. He introduced his fellow students to the game, organized teams, and started developing game rules. He is credited with orchestrating the first organized hockey game in Canada on record, which was in Montreal in 1875.

Creighton participated in nearly every recorded game in Montreal during the first few years it was played. In total, his games on natural ice would not amount to as many games modern players tally during pre-season exhibitions, but they were vital during hockey's embryonic stage. The game quickly caught on, and Creighton is credited with moving the outdoor game into a covered rink in Montreal in 1875 and creating a new activity with nine players per side. The first indoor hockey game was played at the Patinoire Victoria Park in Montreal.

Among Creighton's rules were that the ball could not leave the surface of the ice. This was difficult, so an innovator, he created a wooden puck that was easier to control. He financed his McGill law degree by working in the parliamentary press gallery for The Gazette of Montreal. In 1882, he was appointed Law Clerk of the Senate and split his time between Montreal and Ottawa where he introduced the game to other lawyers.

Creighton played with the Parliamentary and Government House teams in 1889. Among his teammates was the son of the Governor General, Lord Stanley. This team, comprising MPs, senators and aides-de-camp, helped to popularize hockey through exhibition games played in Ontario. The name of their team, coincidentally, was the Ottawa Rebels!

The game of hockey is rooted in a distinct history of honour and nobility, especially in Canada. From the moment the game was introduced, it caught on from coast to coast. People who have played the game know it is the perfect combination of speed, excitement, skill, will, and personal dedication. Many who put on skates for the first time fall in love with the game and before long are passionate about the sport.

Hockey also is a great spectator sport where the fans immediately become part of the action and take stands on which teams and players they like or don't like. There is a personal relationship between fan and player that goes beyond most sports. Perhaps, because the game is played inside on ice, the cheers echo louder as do the boos.

From the minute the first game was played in Montreal in 1875, Canadians have taken ownership of the game. Newcomers to Canada have an immediate liking for the game, as well. Hockey has defined Canada and given Canadians one of its personality traits on the world stage.

Canadians also have an immense emotional attachment to hockey. It has caused riots and played a major role in politics, too. There was the famous riot that took place on March 17, 1955, in Montreal known as the "Rocket Richard Riot." It was an outpouring of emotion that went way beyond the game.

The cause of the riot was the suspension to Montreal Canadiens star player Maurice "The Rocket" Richard. The people of Montreal believed the suspension was more than a penalty imposed on The Rocket; they believed it was an act of prejudice. The NHL was managed by Anglo-Saxons, yet many of the players were from Quebec. The French players in the league, particularly The Rocket, felt that they were treated as though they were second-class citizens. They felt their salaries were lower, and the officiating seemed to discriminate against them. The French players felt they were constantly battling for respect, both on and off the ice. The battle the French players were having on the ice was the same battle the French fans were experiencing off the ice. French Canadians were struggling for respect in Canada while their hockey players were fighting for respect in Canada's game.

The French players, especially The Rocket, were idols of the French Canadian fans, and anything that happened to them every loyal and admiring fan felt, too. They viewed the suspension to The Rocket as the rich, English commissioner ensuring the French, Montreal Canadians would not win the Stanley Cup. The Montreal fans believed that if a star English player, such as Gordie Howe, had committed the same infraction, the same kind of punishment would not have been handed out.

The Rocket was banned from playing in the remainder of the season and all of the playoffs for slashing Hal Laycoe from the Boston Bruins. Laycoe had viciously hit The Rocket over the side of the head with his stick, resulting in a huge gash. The Rocket, the star player in the league, had taken all kinds of abuse during the game and had had enough! He lashed out at Laycoe and started beating him up. When linesman Cliff Thompson tried to intervene, The Rocket threw punches at him, too. To stop the legendary Rocket, opponents would go to any lengths, including tripping, slashing, holding, hooking and general gooning. The referees seemed to turn a blind eye to the abuse the Rocket suffered.

Hal Laycoe was a journeyman player compared to The Rocket. Laycoe's career amounted to the answer to a trivia question: "Who incited the Montreal riots?" The Rocket's suspension went well beyond hockey but struck at the core of racism that appeared to exist in Canada. Hockey was the catalyst for the political protest. The people of Quebec led the protest, not The Rocket. They had had enough, too!

Hockey also was in the middle of the Cold War between North America and the former Soviet Union, which had claimed hockey superiority by continually winning gold medals at the Olympics. The Canadians claimed they only sent amateurs to the Olympics while the Soviet Union sent its best. The Canadians said the USSR would never beat Canada's best.

In September 1972, the Summit Series was set to have the best of the NHL play the Soviet team. The eight-game contest not only put Canadian pride on the line, but for many Canadians it also put the country's lifestyle and belief system to the test. This series made unlikely heroes of people like Paul Henderson, who scored three game-winning goals as well as the decisive game winner in the final game against the Soviets with only a few seconds left. Henderson, who was much more comfortable being out of the spotlight, became an ever-lasting hero from St. John's Newfoundland to Victoria B.C. Everyone in Canada over the age of 50 can remember exactly where they were when Paul scored "The Goal." They can recite accurately what took place when he scored. Henderson's goal saved the integrity and reputation of Canadian hockey. Hockey aficionados love to speculate where Canadian hockey would be had Henderson not scored that goal. Few dispute the entire country would have been in mourning for a long time had Canada lost that game and the series.

On a political scale the games were part of the Cold War with the Soviet Union, and the competition was much more than a series of hockey games. It was good triumphing over evil. It was the conquest of democracy and free thinking over communism and repression. Hockey, again, was the catalyst that brought out myriad of emotions and feelings about who Canadians were and what they believed in. Although the Canadians won the tough and bitter series, Canadians knew their supremacy in the game of hockey was in jeopardy. Our best barely beat theirs. Hockey was now a world game not one owned solely by Canadians.

Hockey has had profound unifying experiences with repercussions well beyond the ice, too, such as when Sydney Crosby scored the overtime goal in the 2010 Vancouver Olympics to win the gold medal.

For Canadian hockey fans, Team USA had replaced the Soviet Union as the hated rival. Most fans less than 50 years old were not aware of the classic matches Canadian teams had played against the mighty Soviet teams. Those epic battles were not part of the new generation's history. Many experts claim the best hockey game ever played was the New Year's Eve game in 1975 between the Montreal Canadiens and the Soviet Army's CSKA team. Although the Canadiens outshot the Soviets 38–13, the game ended in a 3–3 tie. The contest featured great goal-tending, phenomenal defence and sensational end-to-end team play with scoring chance after scoring chance for 60 minutes.

The new generation Canadian fan was focused on beating Team USA in the Olympics. By 2010, the U.S. had developed its hockey programs to the point that it had players that equaled the Canadians. This rivalry was of epic proportions. Team USA and Team Canada games were classic confrontations.

When Team USA forced Team Canada to overtime in Vancouver during the 2010 Olympics championship game, 14 million people—over 40 percent of Canada's population—were glued to their television sets. Canadian pride was on the line again, as this was the first time Canadian pro hockey players were able to compete for the Olympic gold in Canada. When Crosby scored the overtime winner to win the gold medal, a collective sigh of relief swept through the country. There was the same excitement when the Canadian woman's team beat the US woman's team in the gold medal game as well. The cheers in Vancouver echoed coast-to-coast as Canadians had once again defended their game.....both male and female versions.

Canadians set high expectations for hockey players and teams. These expectations have been passed through generations. Canadians idolize their hockey players. Extremely high standards for all participants come with Canadians' romance for hockey. Canadians wanted to see hockey legend and Canadian Bobby Orr fly through the air, scoring his famous overtime goal against the St. Louis Blues in the 1970 Stanley Cup Final to give his team, the Boston Bruins, a sweep and owner-ship of the coveted Stanley cup. Canadians expected his skates to not touch the ice and for him to soar above the rest. The famous picture forever memorializes his flight. For Canadians, Bobby Orr never landed. His flight lives beyond the game.

Canadians want to see their players set examples with their "never quit" attitude. The Canadian way is to approach adversity the way Phil Esposito did in the 1972 Summit Series, Canada vs. USSR series. The Canadians had underestimated the Soviets. After four games were played in Canada, the home team had won only one game, lost two and tied one. This was a disaster for the highly favoured Canadians. The fans expressed their extreme disappointment with their fallen heroes. The great broadcaster Johnny Esaw interviewed Esposito on the ice in Vancouver after the fourth game, who, exhausted and sweaty, chastised the fans for booing Team Canada. "We are here because we love Canada. We are doing our best and we are so disappointed at the booing. If we go to the Soviet Union and their fans boo their players, I'll come back and apologize. This isn't a game. This is war, and we better get ourselves together."

His emotional speech inspired both the Canadian fans and players. It is said that his speech did as much for Canada as Winston Churchill's historic "We shall fight on the beaches" speech, which included the phrase, "We shall never surrender," did for Great Britain, and what Abraham Lincoln's "Gettysburg Address" did for the northern states during the Civil War in United States.

Esposito's speech was brilliant. His words were simple but the meaning was profound. He didn't say to Canada that the professional players were embarrassed by the Soviet team, or that they had underestimated their opponents. He didn't say the scouting reports were inaccurate when they said that Vladislav Tretiak, who continually stonewalled the Canadians in the series, was a weak goalie. (Years later, when Tretiak was inducted into the Hockey Hall of Fame, he was touted as one of the best goalies in the history of the sport. He was so well respected for his goaltending that he was the final torch bearer in the 2014 Sochi Olympics. Later in life he became president of the Ice Hockey Federation of Russia.) What Esposito did say was, that when the chips are down, athletes need to know that their fans are on their side.

The Canadian hockey players had never been in a position like this. They were in uncharted territory. They needed to feel the support of all of Canada to turn things around. Esposito and the others had realized the dream of making it to the NHL, but now their dream had become larger as they were representatives of their country. They carried the hopes, dreams and expectations of all Canada with them on this very important journey. They could not let the dream become a nightmare.

Canadians share the pain with their hockey players and feel their emotions, as they did when Wayne Gretzky was traded from the Edmonton Oilers to the Los Angeles Kings on August 9, 1988. The greatest hockey player at the time—and perhaps of all time—was traded after winning four Stanley Cups in five years. The captain, the heart and soul of the dynastic Edmonton Oilers went from a Canadian team to Hollywood. Canada was shocked, not believing this happened. Peter Pocklington, an entrepreneur and the owner of the Oilers, committed what many believe to be the all-time sacrilegious act in hockey history: trading "The Great One." There have been a few lopsided trades in the NHL, but never has the best player in the sport been cast adrift like a rowboat in a hurricane.

To this day, even though Gretzky admitted he agreed to the trade, fans have not forgiven Pocklington for his ruthless act. In fact, there are those who say that the Oilers, much like the Boston Red Sox when they traded Babe Ruth to the Yankees in 1919, have been cursed and will never win another Stanley Cup until the hockey gods erase the memory of this trade. The general manager of the Oilers at the time, hockey guru Glen Sather, tried to rationalize the trade by saying, "Everything changes. We all get older. We all have more demands on our lives. It's a boy's game that men try to play. This is the tough part of it. We wish Wayne well."

Sather was a brilliant hockey coach and GM, but his insights as a philosopher and visionary were questionable. Canadian fans did not buy his rationalization. The perception was of selfish, rich owners using their players, even the greatest one ever, as nothing but pieces of meat—assets to be dealt at will. There was no loyalty, no respect and no love of the game.

The fans expected Gretzky to rise above it all. He did with his tearful and emotional good-bye to the fans of Edmonton. "The Great One" displayed class that surpassed everyone's expectations. His Edmonton followers were soon joined by admiring fans across Canada and the U.S., heralding him as the greatest ambassador of the game ever. James Creighton would have been proud.

Esposito was right, too. Hockey is more than a game. Hockey is a slice of our life. As players, fans or even casual observers, hockey impacts us in major ways. Visit any rink on any given day and you will see Canadians, whether they be pros, six-year-olds, seventy-year-olds, men or women, who are playing their hearts out. The game defines Canadians. We respect, honour and cherish our game.

CHAPTER 9

THE BROTHERHOOD

The poem "In Flanders Fields" was written by Canadian Lieutenant-Colonel John McCrae during World War I. Two lines from the poem are:

"To you from failing hands we throw / The torch, be yours to hold it high."

This text has been displayed on the archway leading to the ice in the Montreal Canadiens dressing room since 1952. It was inscribed there by Frank Selke Senior, the General Manager of the team at the time. Pictures of legendary players from the Canadiens' storied past proudly surround the quotation. Selke found profound meaning in those words penned by McCrae. In later years, the great Canadian and Montreal goaltender Ken Dryden was cited in a March 17, 1996, Montreal Gazette article as saying the following about the passage in the dressing room:

"Just how different that phrase is from every other team's dressing room, it's not even close. In part, it's the message, although most messages are of similar exhortation. But none of them come from a poem, none of them are that kind of spirit of where the past connects to the present, and the present connects to the future.

"All other phrases are immediate. They're about now, about this team. About this year's team. John McCrae's words are a terrific phrase. They're wonderfully symbolic but they're actually just remarkably accurate and remarkably real."

The Canadiens were so inspired by the poem that during the opening of their new arena, the Bell Centre, that on March 16, 1996, legendary retired players ceremoniously handed a torch to the current players in front of a capacity crowd of 21,288 people plus hundreds of thousands watching on TV. As Dryden said, this was not a symbolic gesture; this was the confirmation of the unity, the bond and the brotherhood that exists within the Canadiens teams, then, now, and into the future. The torch represented the bond between generations of players. That bond enabled the Canadiens to build a dynasty second to none in sport.

In hockey, you will hear that great teams have "a good dressing room," which describes the aura and spirit that is central to the core of the team. Having a good dressing room is more than the players having fun and enjoying themselves, although that is part of it. A good dressing room consists of numerous elements.

Teams that build good dressing rooms have a profound respect and care for and of each team member. Management and players alike must be dedicated to the well-being of each person. The dedication is built on respect for all players as individuals and what they bring to the team. A good team is always more than the sum of its parts, but the parts have to be there. Everyone on the team has a job to do. In hockey, some score the goals, some check the opponents and some keep the puck out of their own net. Without a healthy respect for everyone's contribution, the team will not function properly.

In 1997 the Detroit Red Wings won the Stanley Cup. One of their key players, Russian-born Vladimir Konstantinov, and a few others were involved in a car crash six days after the Red Wings' Stanley Cup victory. They were at a party and decided to take a limo home. The limo driver crashed into a tree. Tragically, Konstantinov was paralyzed for life. The team masseur, Sergie Mnatsakanov, also sustained serious injuries that left him in a coma for a while. The following season the team wore a patch on their sweaters with the word "BELIEVE" written in both English and Russian.

The word "BELIEVE" represented the team's commitment and support for their teammates: the belief that they would get better; the belief that they had a support network; the belief that they would never be alone. Although Konstantinov was never able to play hockey again, the Detroit Red Wings still recognized him as part of their team during their 1998 Stanley Cup win. Normally, players must be part of the active team or have played in a Cup game to have their name engraved on the famous trophy. The Red Wings sought and received special dispensation from NHL Commissioner Gary Bettman to have Konstantinov's name engraved on the Stanley Cup after they won the title. During the celebration on the ice, after winning the Cup game, Vladimir was brought out in his wheelchair to hold the coveted prize. That is the type of respect that builds champions. The respect players have for one another is not something that can be bought. It cannot be bargained for, nor can it be mandated. The respect and camaraderie that is built over time is what enables special teams to achieve special things.

The pillars of respect and caring are critical to teams building dynasties and longevity. When respect and care becomes a given, camaraderie and fun are a natural outcome.. There are many characters and personalities that go into the makeup of any team or organization. Those personalities, naturally, come forward, within the team structure. There will be leaders throughout a team. Some will lead on the playing field, and some will lead off the field. Some will take the spotlight while others earn their keep by winning the battle in the trenches without a lot a fanfare. Others will help build spirit in the dressing room by being able to keep the room fun and reduce tension and stress.

Many pranks are pulled by teammates in all sports. Usually these pranks are not seen by the spectators, but occasionally the fans are let in. In pro hockey, there are a few favourites usually played on rookies. Prior to a game warmup, a rookie needs to be mindful if the team asks him to lead them out on the ice. (The goalies usually lead the team out of the dressing room.) Often when a rookie leads the team out, the rest of the team will not follow and the rookie is left to skate a few laps on his own. Both the fans and the other team enjoy the gag.

You also may occasionally see a game jersey covered in Gatorade because someone has loosened the top of a bottle after the player has had a long shift and wants to get a big drink.

One of the classic pranksters in the NHL was Guy Lapointe of the Montreal Canadiens. Lapointe was renowned for pulling stunts to keep things light. In a November column, Montreal Gazette columnist Dave Stubbs described one of Lapointe's antics when Prime Minister Pierre Trudeau paid a visit to a victorious Canadiens dressing room to congratulate the team. Lapointe coated his palm with Vaseline, and with a firm grip, he slimed the leader of the country.

"He was kind of surprised," Lapointe said grinning. "He laughed. I mean, what are you going to do? Then I gave him a towel."

Hockey seasons are long and demanding, whether it's the beer leagues or the pros. There are battles and confrontations happening on every shift of every game. A good dressing room is essential if the team is going to have the strength to survive these trials and challenges. It is even more important if the team is going to last over time. The players need to feel the support, the caring and the respect from their teammates as well as management. They need to be willing to sacrifice and know others are doing the same for them. Battle pressure needs to be tempered with fun and camaraderie off the playing field.

How did the Rebels manage to survive and stay together so long? They found the formula for longevity in sport. First, they found players who had burning desire to win. They had an intense, internal strength to compete and habitual desire to be the best. They would make personal sacrifices to ensure victory. They would not let the team down. They would not disappoint. They had passion and an undeterred dedication to the team and their teammates. They had each other's backs. They cared about each other. They respected each other. They had confidence in each other. The took care of each other in the trenches.

But they also had fun. They laughed. The seriousness was always coupled with fun and humour. They did not play in the pro leagues. They didn't get financial reward for their efforts. Their rewards came through knowing they gave their best, knowing they gave it all and knowing they played well every shift. Everything mattered. The game mattered, the outcome mattered and their teammates mattered. There were no second chances. They were privileged to wear the sweater, and they knew it.

The Rebels had a robust dressing room full of fun, camaraderie, friendship and devotion. The formula wasn't simple to replicate, but they did it better than most, and they continually did it over the years. That is their legacy. That was their brotherhood.

The incredible story of the Rebels continued to be written. By 2015, the team had turned 46 years old! That's more than four decades of playing the game......
without big salaries, headlines, fame or glory. It was just a bunch of guys playing together for a common purpose. They tackled every obstacle in their way, from leagues folding and not allowing them to play, to teams boycotting them and competing with younger players. From the beginning, when Harry decided to avenge a vicious spear, the Rebels battled and always came out on top. The dream of making it to the big leagues was gone, but their passion gave them the strength and commitment to keep going.

What was the passion? They certainly didn't start out to be the longest lasting non-pro or university team in Canadian history. There was never a thought that one day they would make an application to the Hockey Hall of Fame, let alone be considered for it. There was no fame, and there were no bright lights, as most of the time, except for tournaments, they played in empty arenas in the middle of cold winter nights or early weekend mornings. What inspired this team for 46 years? Their competitive spirit drove them, and their camaraderie kept them coming back.

Although the Rebels loved to compete and enjoyed the fun, there was more than that to their success. They didn't write it down or memorialize it in a formal way; they simply lived a successful formula that made them what they were for all those years.

The Rebels believed in winning. Winning was success. And success was infectious. The Rebels No. 1 rule was play to win. They could be zany, and they could be crazy. They could have lots of fun, but when the puck dropped, it was time to win. Winning was always the goal. Hockey is a game where you keep score—there is a winner and there is a loser. If the goal is to win, then you do the right things to win. You establish a winning climate, you develop winning strategies, and you get everyone pulling in the same direction. With the Rebels, you understood the minute you walked into the dressing room that the goal was to win.

As kids, some of the Rebel players won things, many did not. However, when they became a part of the Rebels, they quickly learned that winning was the DNA. In hockey, as in life, often it is easier to lose than win. Losers place little expectations on themselves. When you're a winner, you have to prove yourself all the time. Winners set the benchmarks. Everyone wants to beat them. The Rebels relished these challenges. For them, when it came to challenges, the bigger the better. They defined themselves by beating the odds. They were tough on those who didn't buy into the winning philosophy, and those individuals soon found themselves on the outside looking in. There were many great hockey players who couldn't cut it with the team because they simply could not take the self-imposed pressure.

Winning is contagious. It permeates throughout an organization. It is a discipline and a commitment to do what it takes to ensure victory. Of course, in hockey, it is critical to keep your body in shape. Though years may had passed, but the Rebels' bodies did not reveal their age. They worked off the ice to stay in playing shape. But more than the physical readiness, they were mentally prepared as well, because every time they stepped on the ice, there was a target on their backs. Their heritage made them the bullseye for 46 years. No matter what league or tournament in which they played, they were always the team to beat.

Most teams eventually fold under that kind of pressure, but with this team, it seemed to propel them forward. The Rebels had confidence that each player would push themselves to the limit. There were no boundaries in their confidence or commitment. The bigger the challenge, the better they would perform. That was a constant with them through four and a half decades.

The Rebels were committed to teamwork. The whole was always bigger than the sum of the parts. Although the players had huge egos, none of them were bigger than the team. Everyone who played for the Rebels was unique in their own way. Some were presidents of companies, some were teachers, some were successful entrepreneurs and others were very successful in a wide array of careers. They all had big personalities. If you were not confident in whom you were, then you would not find a fit with the Rebels. The confidence, though, could never be bigger than the team. No individual, no statistic, or no single accomplishment was bigger than team.

You also had to be tough to be able to withstand the joking, kidding and dressing room pranks. Harry words would often echo, "If you had feelings this was not the team for you."

Over the years the Rebels amassed a very impressive win-loss record. They played 1,840 games, won 1,518 of them, and lost 322. That gave them a winning percentage of 82.5%. So over 46 years, the team won 82.5% of the time! This is an incredible statistic that is unrivalled. The only team that can match it is the New Zealand national rugby team, aka the All Blacks, which won 208 of 244 matches, or 85.2%, from 2000 to 2019. That's a great record over 19 years, but the Rebels kept its pace for 46 years!

The Rebels built on each person's strengths and relied on each other to do what they were good at. The team needed you to do your job. As a player, you knew what your role was, and you wanted to do it well. If you were a scorer, you scored; if you were a bruiser, you hit; if you were a defensive player, you stopped the other guys. Doing what you were good at meant that you fulfilled your role. As part of the team, you were appreciated and recognized for your contribution. No one was more important than anyone else. You felt good about being there, and you never wanted to let your teammates down.

From time to time, when a player had a bad game or just wasn't up to his usual standards for whatever reason, the other players took over. They bailed him out, no questions asked. They covered for him until he got back on track. The expectation was that the player would correct what was wrong and get back to his normal game. Nothing had to be said; it was just done.

February 2020 Team USA celebrated the 40th anniversary of their Olympic Gold medal in men's ice hockey. Team USA in the 1980 Lake Placid Olympics is one of the best examples of the ultimate commitment to teamwork. The "Miracle on Ice" medal-round game during the men's ice hockey tournament will remain one of the biggest upsets in the history of sports. No hockey memoir discussing great teams could ever omit the legendary performance of this group of young men.

Despite the1972 close loss to the Canadian team in the Summit Series, the Soviets were regarded as one of the finest hockey teams in the world. The Soviet "Red Machine" team had captured the previous four Olympic hockey golds, going back to 1964, and had not lost an Olympic hockey game since 1968. From 1956 through 1979, the team took gold at 14 of 23 World Championships. They were undoubtedly the Olympic favourite, expected to win gold in Lake Placid and to set a record for the most consecutive gold medals won by a team in hockey at the Olympics. Back then, NHL players were not allowed to play in the Olympics. The non-professionals from the other teams would stand little chance against the powerful Soviets.

Team USA, however, thought otherwise, and a plan was put in place. The team was led by coach Herb Brooks and assistant coach and assistant general manager Craig Patrick. Brooks coached hockey at the University of Minnesota and had guided the Minnesota Golden Gophers to three NCAA championship titles in 1974, 1976 and 1979 before he was hired to coach the US Olympic team.

He personally picked each player for the team, which included several of his Minnesota players as well as a few from their rival Boston University. The Hall of Fame coach believed the only way to beat the Canadians and the Soviets was to develop a hybrid style of game featuring the speed and puck control of the Soviet game with the creativity and teamwork of the North American game. He stressed peak conditioning, as he believed that the Soviets dominated international competition by exhausting their opponents by the third period.

The "miracle" was not so much that Team USA won gold, but that the management team believed that a bunch of college kids could beat the No.1 team in the world at the Olympic Games. This is the equivalent of taking a group of Canadian University football players and winning the Super Bowl! Everyone scoffed at that suggestion. But not Brooks!

Brooks believed. His belief was that if everyone committed to the same goal, be dedicated to the cause and adhere to the plan, success would be achieved. But there was one more element, and that was to work as a team where the whole was bigger than the sum of the parts.

At a famous turning point in their development, Brooks transitioned the individuals into a team. They were playing an exhibition game in Europe, and the game did not go well. The players were just not coming together. After the final buzzer sounded, Brooks took the USA players back on the ice and started doing a conditioning drill called stops and starts, which is the most hated and exhausting drill in hockey.

Despite the team just having played a game, Brooks ruthlessly skated them round after round of the grueling sprints. It went on for hours. Arena management even turned off the lights to force them to leave.

After each round, Brooks would ask, "Who are you, and who do you play for?" The players had no idea of what he was looking for. Even Patrick wondered what he was up to.

The players were exhausted and confused. They would answer stating their name and school they attended. "I am Mike Ramsey from the University of Minnesota." "I am Dave Silk from Boston University." Then Brooks would skate them again. More players were asked; more answered with their name and school. Drained, off they would go again.

This continued until Mike Eruzione, the captain of the team, finally got it. He stated his name. Brooks asked him, "Who do you play for?" Eruzione proclaimed, "I play for the United States of America." Brooks made his point, the punishing drill ended, and Team USA was formed.

From then on, they became the epitome of teamwork. Each player knew he played for the name on the front of the jersey, not for the one on the back. They also knew that if something special was to happen at these Olympics, it had to be because they played together as a team and not as a bunch of individuals. As individuals they would never beat the best, but as a team, they could achieve their dream. They were dedicated to each other and the team. Some of the players were good enough to make the NHL, but most were just average, and none were stars of the game. But when the 1980 Team USA played together, they reached miraculous levels of performance. They all have a gold medal to prove it, having beaten the Soviet team in the first game of the medal round, and then Finland in the final. The "Miracle on Ice."

The Rebels were very similar. As a team they were much better than the sum of the parts. They were all good hockey players. They all cared for and respected each other, but the team always came first. They were highly intense individuals who were very competitive, yet very committed to the team. Individual stats were never important. Only team results counted.

The Rebels also believed in camaraderie. They carefully selected the players who put on the jersey. Special qualities were needed to be part of the team. There were times when a player just didn't fit the culture. Usually it was not because of their hockey ability, but more their lack of fit as part of the team. When this would happen, they were not invited back to the team the following year, or they would leave of their own accord.

When you were part of the team, however, you were part of the family. You were important, your spouse was important, and your kids were important. The Rebels took care of each other on and off the ice.

Smitty, the one-handed hockey player, later in life was diagnosed with Lou Gehrig's disease. It was painful watching this debilitating disease, to which there still is no cure, take over his body. Smitty fought a brave battle right to the very end. As he was failing, his family decided to have a fund-raising dance in his honour. It would be a chance for him to get together with all his friends and family and to celebrate his life. The funds raised were to help pay for some of the expensive drugs not covered by his health plan. As Smitty was one of the original Rebels and an extremely popular player, the team itself raised close to $5,000. Smitty was overwhelmed by the generosity and outpouring of love from his teammates.

That is what made the Rebels special and differentiated them from other teams. Once you put on the jersey, you were part of the family. On the ice, if an opposing player tangled with one Rebel, he tangled with all of them. No questions were asked; that was just the way it was. This didn't have to be discussed in the dressing room; it was a natural bond that was there. You did what you had to do to keep up your end and never disappoint.

The camaraderie lasted through the decades. The dressing room was always a lively place full of fun, jokes and spirit. This was a retreat, where for a few hours all life's issues went away. Concerns about home or work life disappeared. You may have dragged yourself out of your house on a cold winter night after a long day of work, not quite feeling ready to play hockey, but the minute you walked down the dressing room corridor, you forgot the problems of the day, and your aches and pains diminished. As you opened the dressing room door, whether you were the first guy in or the last, you were revitalized and consumed by the atmosphere.

"Hey, keep your head up tonight, we are playing the team where you speared the guy last game. The guy wants his jock back!"

"Did you hear the one about the guy who found a genie bottle on the golf course…?"

And so it started. The quips went back and forth, and there was laughter, enjoyment and happiness to be part of the team. For the next few hours only hockey and friendship mattered.

During the game the mission was clear: win. Do what you need to ensure the score at the end favours the good guys. Look after yourself, give it all you've got, and take care of the guys wearing the same colour jerseys. Concentrate on the game. Watch the other team to see where their strengths and weaknesses are. Communicate with the others. "Next shift we are out against their gunner, don't let that jerk get to the net. I got the man at the posts, you take the high man in the slot."

The chatter could be heard throughout as the game progressed. Most of the guys played hockey since they were very young. In all those years while on the bench, they probably never once heard anything like, "My teacher didn't give me a good grade on my paper," or "My boss dislikes me." That stuff was saved for later, but was never said during the game.

After the game, it was back into the dressing room for a shower and a beer, thus the name "beer league hockey." For a few minutes they analyzed what went right and what went wrong during the game. The analysis lasted about two minutes, until the cold ones were spread around. Then it was back to the fun and the jokes. Although the game was over, there always were a few good stories to go around about what took place on the ice.

Bruce Wells would chide Rod Farmer, "Hey, what did you do, blow a tire? That number 18 went around you like you were standing still!" Rod would insist that it wasn't his man to cover. They would go at it again and again, one after another, the dressing room antics of post-game quarterbacking and never tire of the great laughs with buddies.

Most nights after the dressing room, it was off to the bar for chicken wings and beer. Clarkson Pump and Patio was their favourite after-hockey pub. "The Pump" was owned by Scott Smith. He was a good, tough hockey player who played a few years with the Rebels before his business duties forced him to retire from the team. The person serving the Rebels' table was always a bright, cheerful young woman who would have the table set awaiting the weekly arrival.

The pub was more than drinking or eating. It was there that decisions were made as to tournaments in which the team would participate, fund raising activities and strategies for approaching the next game. It also was where all issues were discussed: business, government, sports and occasionally personal issues.

After one game, Steve Mauthe was complaining that his daughter just returned from school. She was an excellent figure skater and was trying to earn a spot on the Canadian Olympic team. At the time, Steve was a 30-year veteran of the Rebels. He turned to me, and said, "You need to get your son to take my daughter out for coffee. She is bored and needs to get out." Steve had coached Joe, my son, in midget hockey, so he knew he could trust him with his precious daughter. Little did he know at the time that the coffee date would end with Joe marrying his daughter and them having three children together. It was a new generation of Rebels!

The most intriguing part about the bar however, was how the bill got paid. Some guys would want to share chicken wings, others would want pizza, and a fewer others would want something healthy like a salad. Of course, the bar would have team specials, like a jug of beer and 20 wings at a discounted price.

Not everyone would consume the same amount each week. Separate billing was impossible because of the size of the group, so there was one bill that had to be divided.

These were adult men. Most were married and had kids attending high-ranked universities in Canada or the U.S. All of them had very good jobs or owned their own businesses. The days of being struggling, broke college students were long gone. Dividing and paying the bill each week, however, was painstaking. "I only had 1 glass of beer, Harry had two." "I didn't eat any pizza. I only had 2 chicken wings." Each person paid on the honour system what they thought they should.

After each guy threw in their $10 or $20, there was always a shortfall of at least $50 to $100, not to mention the tip. The soft-hearted Tom Green would make up the shortfall, and everyone would contently go on their way.

I decided this could not continue. It wasn't that Tom could not afford it. Nor did he mind making up the balance. But I felt this simply was not right. I analyzed two weeks of bills, divided the charges by the average number of people who attended the pub each week, added in the tip, and calculated that $30 per player would cover the bill. I also determined that if each player paid $35, a "kitty" could be built to cover a year-end party.

I put this proposal out to the guys. "If you come to the pub after the game, you can drink and eat as much or as little as you wish, but you pay $35 each."

There would be one bill, one collector, and one guy administrating the whole thing. This would be easy, stop all the hassling, and ensure Tom didn't continually overpay. Well, you could have heard the whining from downtown Toronto! "Falcon, you're a crook, this is ridiculous. How big is the mortgage on your home that we are paying for?"

Keep in mind these were the same guys who on the ice would lay their lives down for their teammates. But when it came to paying for chicken wings, the same philosophy eluded them. Strange, how life works. I persisted and prevailed, and the system lived on.

The complaints and whining continued, as well. One night Harry, who was convinced that the numbers just didn't balance, said he would collect the money for the bar bill and prove once and for all that I was scamming my hockey buddies. Everyone drank and ate at will.

At the end of the evening, Harry proudly stood up with his calculator and took the bill. He added the tip, divided it among those who were there and sheepishly proclaimed, "You all owe 35 bucks!" The system worked, but the whining never stopped!

The Rebels believed in leadership and were blessed with great leadership throughout their 46 years. There are many types of leaders, and many situations exist where leaders need to come to the forefront. In a hockey organization, there has to be off-ice leaders—those who step up to get the team organized. They must publish schedules, communicate to the team members, and field questions and phone calls from the players. They must also attend league meetings, collect money and make sure the team is ready to play. Much of this leadership is administrative and thankless. Every team in every sport owes much to those loyal and dedicated few who take on this responsibility.

That leader for the Rebels also made critical decisions about which players would make the cut, what league the team would play in and what the game-day line up would be. Although Harry started the team, Rick McArthur was the person who got the Rebels on the right track.

Rick had amazing leadership skills. He was able to harness a brash bunch of teens and mold them into a cohesive unit able to compete in the Lambton League. Without his yeoman efforts, the team would have been another one of those that survived only a few years. Rick managed the team through the inaugural years in Lambton League.

Once the Rebels were well established, Rick, who was a school teacher, decided to devote his coaching skills to volleyball, and he handed the reins over to Barry Robb. Barry had to stickhandle the team through the transition when the Lambton League folded. He had to research leagues, go to meetings, and in many cases, plead the Rebels' case to gain entry into new leagues.

Barry also had to manage the team through the transition into old-timer hockey. Getting the Rebels entrance into old-timer leagues was a job itself. No old-timer league wanted to let the Rebels in.

Barry and his brother Rick were the founders and proprietors of a very successful pool maintenance business called Aquanaut Pools. They both also were gifted hockey players. It was Barry's leadership and dedication that enabled the Rebels to take the next step in their evolution.

Years later, as the demands and the stress of the pool business increased, Dave Cobban took over the team from Barry. Dave was one of the top real estate brokers in Mississauga. He led the Rebels throughout old-timer hockey. He probably had the toughest job of all, as he, like Barry, had to scout out leagues for the Rebels to play in. He also had to manage the team through a series of health issues as the players aged.

Hockey is a tough game, and the body doesn't heal as quickly as one ages. Dave insisted on a high level of fitness and commitment to play the game, and he led by example. He had great support in his administrative role by Ron Wynne. Ron was a Rebels veteran who had been a leader on the team for over 35 years. Ron, in addition to his great play, was an ambassador for the team. His cerebral nature and great sense of humour were welcome additions to his stalwart play.

None of the players ever questioned the off-ice leaders, as they appreciated the effort and extra time these guys devoted to the team. As important as the off-ice administrative leadership was, there was the on-ice leadership as well. For on-ice leadership, the Rebels relied on each other. Some were scoring leaders, some were defensive leaders, some were strategy leaders and some were inspirational leaders. No one person did it all, and the leadership came when it was needed.

As various situations arose during games, the players never knew who would take charge and lead. One thing that made the Rebels unique was that all the players were leaders in their own way. On any given night, any one of them could have led the team or carried the others on his back, if needed. The Rebels trusted each other to lead. They knew it was never about "I" but always about "we." With the trust came the responsibility that each person had to do his best. They relied on each other, they trusted each other, and they believed in each other. That was powerful leadership.

CHAPTER 10

THE REBEL MAGIC

Commitment to winning, teamwork, respect and camaraderie were the pillars of the Rebels' success and longevity. The pillars were concrete, understood, real and tangible for all the players on the team.

But there was another variable that wasn't quite as clear, concrete or tangible, but it, too, was a major factor in the Rebels' success story. That was the Rebels' magic. There was a magic that surrounded the team. The players knew it existed. They felt it, and more importantly, they believed in it.

It started in the early days of the team. The magic was in their ability to beat the odds and do something beyond the norm. Some would try to define it and make it a understandable. They would say it was their drive and never-give-in attitude. Some would say it was their inability to quit. Others would say it was their capacity to get up after being knocked down. But for the inspirational leaders of the team, they knew that the Rebels had magical powers. They just knew. They didn't need to rationalize its existence.

The first time it was verbalized, the team was playing a game at Lambton Arena. The Lambton games took place early on Sunday mornings. The night before a particular game, there was a party that got pretty wild. The team had decided to go to a dinner show to see King Arthur's Feast at the Constellation Hotel in Toronto. It depicted the days of knights in shining armour. Audience participation was encouraged. In hindsight, this was not a good venue for the likes of the Rebels.

The king's feast setting was certainly one where a big group, like the Rebels, could get a little crazy. Dinner was served on platters, but there were no utensils, so attendees had to eat with their hands. The wine was poured from stone jugs into large goblets.

Nancy, the wife of one of the team's managers, was picked from the audience to act as the king's wife during the show. The actors escorted her back stage and dressed her in a gown that was appropriately suited for the era. A very pretty lady, Nancy filled the part beautifully. She looked stunning under the bright lights on stage. The atmosphere was perfect for all to have a good time. As the food was served and the drinks started to flow, it was clear that this was going to be a memorable night.

Long before the show began, the Rebels and their spouses were well into party mode. When the actual show began, the actors encouraged the audience to get involved. In these kinds of outings, most of the time the audience responds with a polite answer or two, and the show stays on course. With the Rebels in the audience, however, that was not the case, and with "their queen" onstage, they were going to control where this show went!

The restaurant was very generous with the food and drinks, and the stage was set for an uprising.

The Rebels decided they didn't like the king and it was time for a citizen's rebellion. Food started to fly, and before long, the king was arrested and made to stand trial in the Rebels' kangaroo court. The charge against him was he could not satisfy the physical needs of his queen.

The show was out of control. The Rebels had taken over. The audience, as well as the Rebels, were having a ball, as they banished the king and sent him into exile.

The actors themselves seemed to be enjoying a different kind of night at the theatre. A new king was appointed to the throne. An immense man, who was a stranger to the team, was pulled from the audience to be the new "ruler." This gentleman was big enough to have been a lineman from the Toronto Argonauts football team.

The new ruler was a great sport and played along. Perhaps he took his role a little too seriously. When he was asked what he would do to satisfy his new queen, without hesitation he started to describe the night ahead of her. As he eloquently described his plan, management of the restaurant wisely decided to shut the proceedings down and closed the stage lights. The show was over, much to the disappointment of Nancy and the other people in the audience, who were apparently most happy to have the king elaborate further.

Although the show stopped, the partying continued with the cast, the new king and the Rebels. Everything ended very late, yet there was an early morning game yet to play.

For many of the Rebels, the partying must have continued after leaving the hotel because only seven players showed up for the game. This was going to be a tough one. The team had never played with so few players. The seven feared they were going to get killed because they were playing one of the better teams in the league.

As they were getting dressed, the players mostly discussed the night before, as no one really wanted to think about the thrashing they were about to take. Just prior to going on to the ice, however, the guys essentially said, "Look, we have to play this game smart. Let's do the 'rope-a-dope'." Rope-a-dope came from the famous 1974 Rumble in the Jungle fight between George Foreman and Muhammed Ali in Kinshasa, Zaire.

Foreman was heavily favoured to beat Ali. The experts said Ali had no chance against the bigger, stronger, younger Foreman, so Ali decided to use the ropes as a lever, covering up and bouncing off of them while letting Foreman swing to his heart's content. Ali calculated that in doing so, the ropes would absorb much of the force of Foreman's punches. If Foreman kept swinging and Ali kept bouncing off the ropes, eventually Foreman would tire himself out in the heat of Zaire.

The strategy worked. After delivering a constant barrage of punches with seemingly little effect, Foreman was exhausted. Seeing how tired his opponent was, Ali attacked him and knocked him out just prior to the end of the 8th round.

The seven Rebels decided to employ the same strategy: play very defensive hockey, not chase the opponent all over the rink, cover the front of their net and wait for an offensive opportunity.

Sure enough, the other team saw the Rebels were short players and started running at them. Not only were they going to beat them, they were going to punish them, as well. This was payback time. In every game the Rebels played, the other team had a big incentive to beat them. This was now their chance to settle a few scores.

In their over-exuberance, however, the opposing team started to take penalties. The Rebels took advantage on the power play and scored: 1–0 Rebels. The other team thought it was no problem. They were all over the Rebels, and they figured it was just a matter of time.

The Rebels played defence perfectly. All of a sudden, a blocked shot and breakaway for the Rebels made the game 2–0! Going into the third period the guys from the other bench were yelling at each other, "C'mon, this is embarrassing they only have seven guys."

That was all the Rebels needed to hear. The strategy was working. Their opponents were frustrated and trying too hard, and they started doing dumb things. Of course the Rebels, seeing the end in sight and tasting victory, started to play more aggressively and pushed the play, making it even tougher on the opposition. The adrenaline was flowing. Game over. The Rebels won 4–1.

There could have been references made to the Rebels' rope-a-dope, or the players could have called themselves the Magnificent Seven, but as they triumphantly walked into the dressing room, one of the guys shouted, "That was magic!" Rebels magic was born!

The magic continually, enveloped the Rebels. It characterized their game. It was always there helping them to beat the odds as well as teams who were younger, faster or more talented. The magic was there to overcome obstacles that stood in their way. The magic was there to help them win when the prospect looked impossible. The magic was in the sweater. The players felt it. The sweater was their armor. They were knights seeking their next adventure. There was nobility in the cause and no challenge that was too big. No mountain was too large to climb. They were Don Quixote on skates, "…willing to march into hell for a heavenly cause." On game day, with the jersey on, no matter what was happening with the individuals prior to the game, no matter what antics were going on in the locker room, it was crunch time. They were enveloped in magic and were invincible.

The Rebels' formula was not a simple one, but the players followed it, and it helped them to deliver 46 years of excellence. The formula was: playing to win, and committing to make winning a lifestyle; putting the team first and tucking away egos and personal agendas; vehemently caring for fellow teammates and building camaraderie; playing with the confidence that teammates had your back; and knowing with the jersey on, there was magic.

CHAPTER 11

GAME WITH NO END

For 46 years the Rebels had been playing hockey together in leagues throughout Toronto. The Centennial League in Etobicoke was their final stop. They were still having a great time playing the game they loved. They competed successfully and more than held their own against teams much younger than them. In their 46th year they finished in second place just a few points away from first during the regular season. The first round of the playoffs was not going to be an easy one. The Rebels were going to face a team that had only been in the league a year. They also happened to be the youngest team in the league. Although they respected the Rebels they had no desire to lose to "the old guys." To make it worse for the Rebels, the new team had a couple of ex-pros on their roster. Both were excellent players and one had scored 50 goals for the Toronto Maple Leafs, just a few years back. The format of the semi-final game was a one game show-down with the winner moving on to the finals.

In the pre-game warm up it was evident the young guys were very confident. They zipped around the ice surface yelling and banging their sticks as they loosened up for the game. No doubt their goal was to intimidate the Rebels and take control of the game early. The young guys were letting the old guys know who was in charge. Over the years the Rebels had seen this type of behaviour many times before. An all too familiar story.

The Rebels were ready and they weren't going to be intimidated. They knew they could not out-skate the young guys, especially when they were fresh at the beginning of the game. The Rebels would have to play their masterful puck control game and slow the pace down, if they had any chance of winning. Their experience would level the playing field.

At the beginning of the game the young guys did take control keeping the play in the Rebels end. The ex-pros seemed to be taking it easy thinking this game was going to be a walk-over. After a few minutes of play the score was 1-0 for the young guns. The Rebels kept their cool and continued to play their game. The Rebels always would rely on a basic rule of hockey, the puck can move faster than a player can skate. From the time a youngster holds a hockey stick in his or her hand, coaches teach them that no matter how fast you skate, the puck can always move faster. The Rebels were masters at letting the puck do the work and making the other team chase it and them around. Much to the delight of the former Rebels who were in the stands watching the game, the Rebels puck control started to frustrate the young guns. Even the ex-pros were surprised. In doing so the Rebels continued to play smart and kept the game close. By the time the third period started the game was only 1- 0 for the young guys. The Rebels strategy was working.

The third period was crunch time. The Rebels kept control of the puck and the young guns were tiring and started to slow down. They became even more frustrated and started to take a few penalties. With two minutes left to play in the game the young guys dumped the puck into the Rebels' end of the ice. Wells raced to the corner to retrieve it. One of the young guns was chasing him trying to stop Wells from getting control. By the way he was chasing him it appeared the he was lining him up for hard check into the boards. Surely, he wasn't going to pull a stunt like that in a non-contact old-timer game....was he?

The number of nasty and dirty plays in hockey is countless. In many cities, small towns and communities, hockey games are played every winter night. They are played all over the world in countries like Canada, Denmark, France, Finland, Italy, Norway, Russia, Sweden, Switzerland, and the USA. On any given night, someone, whether it is a young kid or a professional, is delivering a cheap shot to someone else with a dirty play. It happens all the time. Some will argue that it's part of the game, while others will say it's simply the nature of the competition. Hockey elite will argue that the pace of the game is so fast that reactions happen instinctively. Throughout time, inexplicable cheap shots that go beyond imagination occasionally have occurred, even at the professional levels.

The stick over the head that Maurice "The Rocket" Richard suffered at the hands of Hal Laycoe (see Chapter 8) certainly rates as a classic. Probably the worst incident in all professional hockey history was the 1969 Ted Green and Wayne Maki incident. Green, a well-established veteran tough guy in the league, played for the Boston Bruins; Maki was a rookie with the St. Louis Blues trying to make the team. The late broadcaster Dan Kelly once referred to the 1969 stick-swinging battle between the two as "one of the most horrifying, most violent exchanges I've ever seen in hockey."

It happened on September 21 during a pre-season game in Ottawa. Kelly was calling the play-by-play for a St. Louis radio station that night. Early in the game, Green and Maki collided in the Boston zone. Linesman Ron Finn, officiating in only his fourth NHL game, was close by when the two players collided. He could feel the breeze when Green turned and viciously swung his stick at Maki, missing him by a few inches. Maki retaliated quickly, swinging his own stick and hitting Green on his head.

Helmets were not generally worn then, and Green dropped to the ice. He was motionless, barely conscious and groaning. When he tried to get up, he was like a newborn deer, stumbling over his feet. The injury was life threatening, and he was lucky to survive. In 1971, Green returned to hockey with a steel plate in his head and played for nearly another decade.

Maki's career was cut short, as a few years later he was diagnosed with a brain tumor, from which he eventually succumbed.

Anyone who has ever played hockey knows that the two cheapest of cheap shots are the spear and the butt-end. The spear is when the blade of the stick is jabbed, generally at the groin or stomach area of an opponent, which can cause major organ damage because of the vulnerability of those areas of the body. The butt-end is when the end of the stick is jabbed at an opponent's head, face or chest, again usually causing great injury because of the velocity and bluntness of the blow. Hockey players know these infractions are off limits. If they do occur, the penalties and possible retaliation are very severe as these infractions violate the unwritten code of the game.

In old–timer hockey, no one would ever expect one of these cheap shots, so when the young gun gave Wells a butt-end in the face while fighting for the puck, the referee immediately blew his whistle and the game came to an abrupt stop. The Rebels were afraid that something was going to erupt. Wells, of all guys, was not one to let this pass unpunished. The team froze in their tracks when they saw the blood spewing from Well's eyelid. The players on both benches were on the edge of their seats as Wells skated up to the young punk. Everyone was expecting a bench brawl, but instead, Wells tapped him on the pads holding his stick with one hand while holding his face with the other. He seemed to be saying, "It's OK, I know it was an accident." But it was not accident: The punk gave him a cheap shot. Both teams and the referees knew it.

Well's gestured to the Rebels' bench with his hand, clearly giving the sign to calm down. That was not typical behaviour for Wells or for the Rebels. The former pros on the other team looked relieved that this didn't develop into something greater. The Rebels too were amazed that Wells had the control to take the high road.

As Wells spoke we could hear the ghost of Herb Brooks: "....but not tonight." As the Rebels looked down their bench, it was as though they were 18 again. The white hair and wrinkles were gone. They were back at Lambton Arena on a cold Sunday morning, a bunch of kids looking at each other, grinning with expectation. They were young and full of exuberance. They had gotten their revenge on Gary G 46 years ago. This was a night for magic.

With the young guys penalized, the next few minutes were now under Rebels control. The Rebels scored immediately on the power play to tie the game. With less than a minute remaining, Dave Cobban did what he did best, he took the team on his back. This was no longer a game at Centennial arena in the middle of the night, this was the finals in the Olympics or maybe the 7th game of the Stanley Cup finals. For the Rebels, on this night, there was no difference. With only a few seconds left in the game, Dave picked up the puck from the face–off. He danced past the defenseman and was headed on a breakaway. He swooped in from the left and drove to the net. The goalie came forward to cut down the angle. Dave faked a shot and then deked. The goalie anticipated the play and moved with him. A puck weighs 6 ounces, is 1 inch thick and has a diameter of 3 inches. There was exactly that amount of space open in the top corner of the net. Dave went for it. Time stood still.

There is nothing as eerie as the silence that is created when sport fans hold their breath during a thrilling play, like this one. Both teams waited to see if the puck would go into the net or find its way into the goalie's immense glove. The silence that filled the arena was the same as the one that consumed the Toronto Skydome when the line drive that Toronto Blue Jays' Joe Carter hit in the 1993 World Series game was heading for the fence. It was game six against the Phillies.

Toronto was leading the series three games to two, but trailing 6-5 in the bottom of the 9th. The Jays' Rickey Henderson and Paul Molitor were on first and second base. Carter was at the plate. Philadelphia's Mitch Williams, known as "The Wild Thing," whose save record in the post-season was a perfect 4-0, was pitching. The count on Carter was 2-2.

Joe lined the next pitch towards the left field fence. The crack of the bat silenced the crowd of over 55,000 who stood holding their breath waiting to see whether the ball would sail over the fence and land in fair territory. That short burst of silence defined one of the greatest memories in Toronto sports history. The roar that followed seconds later was heard around the baseball world. The late Tom Cheek, the famous television and radio announcer, proclaimed "Touch 'em all Joe! You'll never hit a bigger home run in your life."

Cobban's shot headed for the top of the net. The benches stood silent. The ping of the puck hitting the crossbar could be heard throughout the arena. Then the Rebels erupted in thunderous cheers. The puck bounced off the crossbar into the net! The Rebels won. It was magic! The Rebels stormed onto the ice to hail their hero...... "Not tonight." On to the Championship!

The young guns were shocked that they lost the game. "How do the Rebels do it? Every year they beat the odds and end up playing for it all," was the sentiment echoed from the young team as they shook hands at the end of the game. As they skated off the ice there was the aura of surprise and respect for the oldest team in the league. The only ones not surprised were the Rebels. They understood the magic.

As the Rebels were celebrating in the dressing room after the game, they barely heard the door open as the league President had come in. Once he got everyone's attention, which was not easy, the partying stopped and he began to speak. Typically the team was expecting him to outline the time of the championship game the following week. He would congratulate the team and wish them good luck.

This year however was different. The President, who was also a player in the league seemed stuck for words. "Guys, I am embarrassed to tell you but we overbooked our schedule. The City needs to remove the ice because they are having problems with the refrigeration system. The arena is not available for a game next week. That means we either cancel the final game or play the it in another arena."

The Rebels were not interested in playing the game in another arena. The other team they were to match up with, felt the same way. It was decided to let the season end without a championship game. There is always supposed to be a winner declared at the end of the season in any sport. The best team does not always come out on top but nonetheless there is always a winner declared. A season cannot simply end without a winner. There always has to be the summit, the culmination and the crowning. There always has to be the thrill of victory and the agony of defeat.

CHAPTER 12

THE SWEATER

So the 46th season of Rebels hockey came to an unpredictable end. No championship game and no crowning of the top dog. The team decided to rent ice and have Year-end skating party where a team photo could be taken. The fun skates were welcome because the guys could bring their hockey playing sons, daughters or in some cases grandchildren to play with the team. The Rebels were out in full force and many of the their kids came out as well. The skate seemed to have a celebratory feel about it, despite not playing a final game. Of course after the skate there would be the traditional visit to the Pump restaurant to have a few refreshments and the regular feast of chicken wings. No doubt there would be robust discussions about summer plans, how the season ended and naturally, how to split the bill.

At the Pump, crazy Harry and I ended up sitting at the same table. Not too many people were paying attention to us as there were many different conversations taking place. I commented that this was a particularly rewarding season, even though it didn't end as anticipated. "The team played really well all year against some very stiff competition. We are getting older and the league is getting younger and better." Harry was an unpredictable and zany guy but when it came to the team he founded, he was always very protective. Harry's view of the season's end was quite unique and very different from the rest of the guys, who were disappointed that there was not a championship game. He said, "You know Falcon, I found this ending quite appropriate. I am not sure how much longer we can keep competing against the younger guys but if our competitive days are over, this would be the perfect ending." He explained further, "Look, we have played for 46 years, we have won more games and championships than any team I can think of. We have beaten some great hockey teams who had rosters filled with ex-pros and great players. We have been loved and we have been hated but no matter what, everyone we played against respected the Rebels.

I am glad the season didn't end. We are just a bunch of ordinary guys who have given everything we had to this game and this team. What we brought to this game should never end. In fact there should never be an end for those in any sport who got passed over and never made it to the big leagues. Those people who have the competitive spirit and the conviction to play simply for the love of the game and not for the money, notoriety or fame are the ones who keep sports going. They are the true champions. What we have left unfinished is for all those who know who they are, have no delusions of fame or glory, but still give it all they have to make every moment count, to complete. That's what made getting up early in the mornings or playing late at night in dingy, cold arenas in front of empty seats all worthwhile. What we did matters."

I am not sure if Harry realized in those few words how he so eloquently summed up the 46 years of the Rebels. The Rebels had something special driving them. Not even the Pros had what they had. Some who made it had great careers, unfortunately however, the game almost ruined others. Derek Sanderson was able to pull his life back together and fortunately his story can end well. The same was not true for countless others where the demands of the game and its' lifestyle were too much to handle. There are too many stories about fallen athletes, whose lives were absorbed by drugs, alcohol and abuse. Often there is a fine line between the dream and the nightmare. The Rebels on the other hand were able to build a team, a spirit, a lifestyle and a sense of belonging that is the example of why playing sports is important, even if you don't get to the top. Every kid who never makes it should learn from this example.

Not that playing in the Pros is a bad thing. There are many Pros who have fabulous careers and great lives. Just by making it to the Pros you are the exception. Living the dream is the exception. The Rebels were able to carve out their own dream. Average people creating something so extraordinary it transcended decades. What Harry was saying is that every amateur in any discipline should learn from the Rebels. The dream doesn't have to end with the "good enough speech." The dream doesn't have to end in disappointment and loss. There are many unsung heroes throughout many disciplines in life, whose journey should be celebrated

The Rebels started as a bunch of high school kids. Harry gave them a purpose, albeit a bizarre motive for revenge on a deserving culprit. His recruitment process zeroed in on young men who all had humble backgrounds, all loved the game of hockey and at one point all had shared the dream. Somewhere they all shared the "not good enough chat," and they all had something to prove to themselves. None of them would let their dreams end there. They were Rebels at heart. When they came together they started to build a bond that distinguished them. As time progressed they built a reputation and legacy that differentiated them from the rest. They would not be beat. The magic they created was compelling. As others joined they were immediately bought into the culture and became part of the legacy. They were an unequalled dynasty in the making.

The Rebels were more than a team. They were family. They created a culture of caring, sharing and brotherhood. Each and every player had their own story of what brought them to the Rebels. Each player had their own reasons why they continued to play for decades together. Each player contributed to the success of the team and made the Rebels special.

Over time the Rebel story continued to grow. The young kids turned into adults and eventually had their own families. The Rebel family was part of theirs. You could not tell where one family ended and the other started. The Rebels were part of the fabric of the players lives. Over more time as the Rebels graduated into old-timer hockey their reputation as an unbelievable hockey team was firmly established but at the core of their greatness was the unbreakable Rebel spirit. The players had the heart but the team had the soul. Their force was undaunted.

Over time the team created a life that went well beyond the sport. When you walked through the dressing room door, year after year, you knew you were home. No matter where we were, no matter what jokes and pranks were pulled, no matter what decade we were in, when it was game day and the Rebel jersey was pulled on, we became 18 years old again - serious, proud, committed and above all else defiant.

As the evening at the Pump came to a close, we headed out to our cars to go home. Jake and Bryce, two of my young grandchildren, who were with us at the Pump came over to my car to say good-bye. I was parked between Harry's car and Ernie's. Just then Harry opened up the trunk of his car and took his Rebel sweater out of his bag, He asked for Ernie's as well. Ernie joked and asked if Harry was going to frame them in his home. Harry smiled took the sweaters and handed them to the <u>two</u> kids saying, "Keep them, they are magic." The kids were thrilled to have the jerseys. Harry looked at the youngsters and smiled; "Carry the torch high."

EPILOGUE

On Saturday, Sept. 21, 2019, the Rebels had a 50th anniversary banquet to celebrate their longevity and accomplishments. The party was held at The Oakville Pump & Patio in Oakville, Ontario. The players' spouses, family members and friends also came to mark the occasion. It was a grand gala that the team embraced.

Molson Coors Canada and The Oakville Pump & Patio sponsored a huge banner that hung in the venue's entrance way congratulating the Rebels on this significant milestone, and everyone enjoyed a fabulous feast, colourful decorations, old Rebel sweaters and vintage pictures of Rebels from past events. Family and friends had fun trying to identify players in pictures from 50 years ago. Of course, none would acknowledge that they had changed at all! That was the Rebel way.

All kinds of stories were told, and lots of reminiscing about the Rebels' 50 years took place. Catherine Holland from the Mississauga Sports Council delivered a congratulatory message from the council. Harry accepted the council's congratulations and addressed the team, saying, "Never in my wildest dreams did I think I would be standing in front of you 50 years later. I am not sure what drove us or why we did it, but I sure am thankful that we did."

Before the partying and dancing began, I ended the formal part of the evening with a tribute to the team, saying, "The Rebels are an anomaly in senior ice hockey. There will probably never be a team like this again. Although Harry is not sure what drove us or why we did it, I do know: We did it for the love of the game and all the things that went with it, the camaraderie, the friendships, the competition, the fun, the feeling of worth and the brotherhood. We did it because we created something special. There is no end in sight for us. Even though we do not play competitively anymore, we still gather, have an occasional skate, play some golf and still revel in each other's company. 50 years is not an end but a beginning for more to come not only by us but all those who continue their journey long after the Pros said no. Congratulations on our 50 years!"

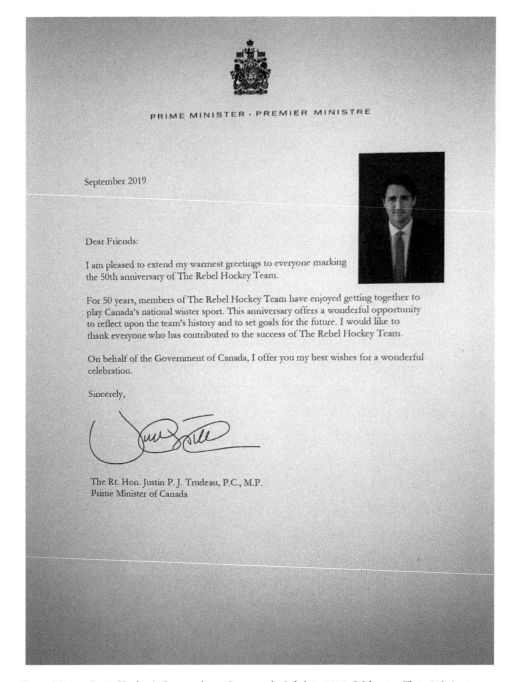

PRIME MINISTER · PREMIER MINISTRE

September 2019

Dear Friends:

I am pleased to extend my warmest greetings to everyone marking
the 50th anniversary of The Rebel Hockey Team.

For 50 years, members of The Rebel Hockey Team have enjoyed getting together to
play Canada's national winter sport. This anniversary offers a wonderful opportunity
to reflect upon the team's history and to set goals for the future. I would like to
thank everyone who has contributed to the success of The Rebel Hockey Team.

On behalf of the Government of Canada, I offer you my best wishes for a wonderful
celebration.

Sincerely,

The Rt. Hon. Justin P. J. Trudeau, P.C., M.P.
Prime Minister of Canada

Prime Minister Justin Trudeau's Congratulatory Letter to the Rebels in 2019 Celebrating Their 50th Anniversary

The Rebels original team members in 1969.
Bottom Row L - R: Bob Falconi, Tom Bolko, Tom Goalie, John Good, Brian Smith
Top Row: "The Kid" (Asst Manager), John Cottrell, Rick Osborne, Terry Lavarue, Gord Chalmers,
Mario Caranci, Tony Caranci, Tom G, Wayne Magee, Harry Mellon, Manager John G.

WORKS CITED

"Archival Collections Catalogue." *Manuscript of In Flanders Fields and Other Poems*, 1970.
   https://archivalcollections.library.mcgill.ca/index.php/manuscript.

Gladwell, Malcom. *Outliers: The Story of Success.* New York City: Little, Brown and Company, Hachette Book Group, 2011. Print.

Sanderson, Derek, and Shea, Kevin. *Crossing The Line: The Outrageous Story Of A Hockey Original.* Chicago, Triumph Books, 2012. Print.

ACKNOWLEDGEMENTS

I would like to thank Glynis Gibson from Gibson Communications, my editor, who took my words and concepts and helped to transform them into what is presented in this book. Thanks Glynis.

More importantly, I want to thank all my Rebel friends whom I have had the pleasure to not only play hockey with for 46 years, but also to grow up with. We started as teens and grew into men. We were zany and crazy, but we learned and matured together. My association with them shaped my life and helped me to become the person I am today. By being part of the Rebels, I learned how to win like a champion, and how to lose like one, too. I learned the importance of being a teammate who was willing to sacrifice my personal agenda for the good of the team. And I learned how to face challenges, fears and adversity with confidence, humour and resilience.

I was one of those guys who was given the "not good enough" speech in the smoky office when I was young, but thanks to the Rebels, I learned that simply playing for the love of the game might have been a bigger reward.

I also learned with the Rebels that on game day, when we pulled the sweaters over our heads, we could be 18 years old again, when magical things happened.

Thank you, my friends.

#27

CPSIA information can be obtained
at www.ICGtesting.com
Printed in the USA
BVHW020031290421
605774BV00002B/2